FROM BISMARCK
TO ADENAUER

hαRpeR ✦ τοRchbooks

*A reference-list of Harper Torchbooks, classified
by subjects, is printed at the end of this volume.*

FROM BISMARCK
TO ADENAUER

Aspects of German Statecraft

Revised Edition
GORDON A. CRAIG

HARPER TORCHBOOKS
The Academy Library
HARPER & ROW, PUBLISHERS
New York, Evanston and London

TO MY MOTHER

Jane Morton Craig

FROM BISMARCK TO ADENAUER

© 1958 by The Johns Hopkins Press, Baltimore 18, Md.
Revised edition © 1965 by Gordon A. Craig.
Printed in the United States of America

This book originated as The Albert Shaw Lectures on Diplomatic History given in 1958, and was first published by the Johns Hopkins Press in 1958. It is here reprinted by arrangement. Dr. Craig has revised the book for the Torchbook edition.

First HARPER TORCHBOOK edition published 1965 by
Harper & Row, Publishers, Incorporated
49 East 33rd Street
New York, N.Y. 10016

Library of Congress catalog card number: 58-59683.

CONTENTS

PREFACE TO THE TORCHBOOK EDITION

IN THEIR ORIGINAL form, the chapters that make up this book were delivered at The Johns Hopkins University in March 1958, as the Albert Shaw Lectures in Diplomatic History, and published in the following year by the University Press. Much has happened since that time, both in the world of politics and in that of scholarship, and I have taken advantage of the appearance of the Torchbook edition to make a thorough revision of the whole text and bring the documentation up to date. The most significant changes and additions have been made in the later chapters, for reasons that are obvious, and the chapter on Konrad Adenauer, while retaining its original form, has been completely redone.

As in the Preface to the original edition, I should like to express my gratitude to the members of the Department of History of The Johns Hopkins University for inviting me to give the Albert Shaw Lectures, and also to acknowledge my debt to all those who gave me criticism and assistance during the period of their composition. These include Elmer A. Beller, Jerome Blum, E. Harris Harbison and J. R. Strayer of the Department of History of Princeton University; the late Frederick S. Dunn and Klaus Knorr of the Center of International Studies of that university; Hildor A. Barton, Major A. F. Hurley USAF, Philip Kolody, Daniel M. Lewin, Lt. Colonel Wallace C. Magathan USA, and R. L. Chambers, who were the members of my graduate seminar in German history at Princeton University in 1958; and Gabriel Almond, Hans W. Gatzke, Felix Gilbert, Victor Lange and the late Theodor E. Mommsen.

To Wolfgang J. Helbich, formerly a member of my Princeton

seminar and now *Wissenschaftlicher Rat* at the University of Heidelberg, I owe a particular debt, because in the course of translating the
original text for the German edition of 1961 he discovered a number
of passages in which fact had been either misstated or strained. His
corrections have been incorporated here.

Finally, I have been aided in the preparation of this new edition
by discussions with my colleagues at Stanford University and the
Free University of Berlin, particularly Reinhard Bendix, Walter
Bussmann and Hans Herzfeld. I should like to thank them too.

G. A. C.

Berlin-Dahlem, June 1964

INTRODUCTION TO THE TORCHBOOK EDITION

IN APRIL 1964, in an address in New York in which he formulated the fundamental principles of American foreign policy in the nuclear age, President Lyndon B. Johnson warned his audience against the twin dangers of rigidity and over-confidence. "Foreign policy," he said, "is more than a list of general principles. It is the delicate job of adjusting these principles to specific dangers and possibilities. To it belongs a knowledge of one's strength and an awareness of one's limitations in any new situation. . . . In the face of unpleasant facts, simple historical observations or the application of general rules are of little help. What is required is concrete measures—as well as courage, intelligence, and restraint."

This passage from the President's speech was reprinted in all of the major newspapers of Western Germany.[1] and it was appropriate that it should have been. For, despite the fact that Germany began its career as a united nation under the leadership of a man who would have subscribed whole-heartedly to President Johnson's statement—namely, Otto von Bismarck—it has nevertheless given the world since his time two illustrations of the drastic results that can follow from failure to recognize the limits imposed by reality upon a nation's foreign policy.

It may well be that the lack of restraint that involved Germany and the world in two destructive wars had its roots in the frustrations of German history, in the long years of humiliation when Heinrich Heine could accurately describe the relative strength of the European powers in the jeering lines.

> Russia and France control the land,
> Great Britain rules the sea.
> Ours is the misty realm of dreams
> Where there's no rivalry.

[1] In some cases, the whole address was printed. See *Frankfurter Allgemeine Zeitung*, 22 April 1964.

It is doubtless true also that German headstrongness and lack of mod-
eration in political thought and action was influenced by the lack of
political experience and perspective which resulted from the survival
in Germany of an absolutist form of government for more than a century after the other great nations of the west had turned to liberalism
and democracy. The historian Gervinus wrote in 1849 that since they
were denied any share in the political life of their country, Germans
tended "to flee from real life into the ideal, to sacrifice the sound
beat of instinct to excessive intellectual acrobatics and introspection,
and to weaken their ability to recognize the real by absorption in
chimerical fantasies." When, however, these "heroes of the word"
were galvanized into action, Gervinus added, both their ambition
and their rage when it was baulked tended to be excessive, and
they were prone to forms of behavior that no one "thinking of the state
of our cultural development and domestic virtues" would have thought
possible.[2]

German history since Gervinus's time has in large part been an
elaboration of this statement, and the story of German statecraft, in at
least one of its aspects, is the story of the failure of those who had
the clearest appreciation of international realities to restrain the head-
long thrust to the utmost that periodically marked the behavior of
the ruling elite, the special interest groups, the intellectuals ("heroes
of the word"), and even the German masses.

In the first stages of his ministerial career, during the Austrian
and French wars, Bismarck found that both his moderate objectives
and the security of his country were jeopardized by official and public
pressure for a *guerre à l'outrance*, followed by a draconian and bound-
lessly lucrative peace;[3] and during the 1870's and 1880's his direction
of policy was always complicated by the necessity of resisting the
influence of individuals and groups whose sense of measure and recognition of the limits of foreign policy were less developed than his
own. On the whole, Bismarck had his way, but it cannot be said
that his success or the example he provided of what great gains can
be made by cautious and systematic diplomacy made much impression
on his country. Certainly they made none on the ruler who in the

---

[2] Georg Gottfried Gervinus, *Shakespeare* (Leipzig, 1849), quoted in Walter
Muschg, "Deutschland ist Hamlet," *Die Zeit*, 1 May 1964.

[3] See Gordon A. Craig, *The Politics of the Prussian Army, 1640-1945*
(Oxford, 1955), chapter 5.

end dismissed him, William II, who regarded prudence and system as un-German flabbiness[4] and preferred a diplomacy characterized by dramatic gestures and shows of force. The almost neurotically violent nature of Wilhelmine statecraft, while failing to achieve its purposes, aroused general fear and suspicion of Germany and contributed in no small measure to the coming of war in 1914. At the same time, the romantic dream of European domination that was shared by so many Germans before 1914, and which assumed cruder forms after hostilities began,[5] not only helped to prolong that conflict but made severe peace conditions inevitable when the German armies finally collapsed.[6]

In the post-war years, German foreign affairs were conducted, at least for a time, in a safer and saner manner. Traditional diplomacy, with its sense of proportion and its recognition of limitations, came into its own again and found at least one gifted practitioner in Gustav Stresemann. But the effectiveness of his efforts to solve national problems by peaceful negotiation was blunted by lingering Allied suspicion of Germany's reliability, and this distrust found its justification in clear evidence that Stresemann's policies did not enjoy the support of large, and dangerously bellicose, groups within his own country. It is doubtful whether Stresemann could long have withstood the agitations of those elements even if he had not died in 1929. His successors in the last years of the Weimar Republic found it necessary to trim their sails to the rising winds of virulent nationalism; and before long German policy was in the hands of Adolf Hitler, who recognized no limits whatsoever, and whose grandiose ambitions led to a second German disaster more frightful in its scope than the first.

The pages that follow are not intended as a comprehensive discussion of the forces that have determined the evolution of modern Germany, nor do they pretend to give a circumstantial account of Germany's diplomatic history in the last one hundred years. Their

[4] See *Die Grosse Politik der Europäischen Kabinette, 1871-1914: Sammlung der diplomatischen Akten des Auswärtigen Amtes* [hereafter cited as G. P.] (Berlin, 1921 ff.), XXIV, 116, and E. L. Woodward, *Great Britain and the German Navy* (Oxford, 1935), pp. 172 ff.

[5] See Fritz Fischer, *Griff nach der Weltmacht* (Düsseldorf, 1962), chapters 1, 2 and *passim*.

[6] See Hans W. Gatzke, *Germany's Drive to the West: A Study of Germany's Western War Aims during the First World War* (Baltimore, 1950).

purpose is rather to examine the ways in which foreign policy has been conducted in Germany: the aims and the methods of the nation's leading statesmen, their problems and their success or failure in dealing with them, and the part played by their diplomacy in Germany's tragic progress from the security of Bismarck's Reich to the divided and vulnerable nation of the present day. They end with what, in the light of the present state of the documentation and our nearness to the events, must be considered a highly tentative appraisal of the diplomacy of Konrad Adenauer, of whom it can at least be said that he profited from reflection upon his country's past, that he steadfastly set his face against the delusions to which his countryman had so often been inclined, and that his own statecraft embodied the virtues emphasized by President Johnson in New York.

chapter one

BISMARCK:

Diplomacy as a Vocation

IN FEBRUARY 1847 a young woman named Johanna Puttkamer sent a letter to her fiancé in which, yielding to the literary taste of the day, she wrote the words, "Loyalty is the very fire that always vivifies and sustains the heart of existence." The recipient of this communication, a Pomeranian squire with modest holdings at Schönhausen, repeated this sentence in his reply and remarked that it struck him as being "one of those nebulous, misty phrases from which it is difficult to derive any clear meaning and which not infrequently have injurious results when they are carried over from poetry to actuality—especially by women who as young girls have observed life almost exclusively through the spectacles of the poet."[1]

This was perhaps less than ardent; but then not even love should be allowed to excuse bad prose, and this unfeeling East Elbian landholder was never one to tolerate the inflated phrase. Twenty years after this time he was making even unkinder comments about the stylistic flights of envoys of the Prussian crown and counsellors in the Foreign Ministry, complaining that their dispatches were marked by "pompous phraseology" or "cheap bombast,"[2] and rejecting their drafts

[1] *Fürst Bismarcks Briefe an seine Braut und Gattin,* edited by Fürst Herbert Bismarck (Stuttgart, 1900, p. 34).

[2] Fritz Hartung, "Bismarck und Arnim," *Historische Zeitschrift,* CLXXI (1951), 51.

because they were cacophonous[3] or burdened down with meaningless superlatives.[4] It was not, in fact, easy to meet the literary standard set by Otto von Bismarck.

Bismarck's critical qualities were put to full use in the first years after he became Minister President and Foreign Minister of Prussia in 1862. He inherited a diplomatic service which, although it had been founded by Frederick William I, enjoyed little prestige in the country. This was due partly to the military traditions of the Prussian state, where it was infinitely more glamorous to wear the King's coat than to indite dispatches, and partly, and perhaps more, to the timid and vacillating nature of Prussian foreign policy during the first sixty years of the nineteenth century, which was hardly designed to attract spirited and talented young men. Filled with mediocre minds, and lacking the kind of diplomatic tradition that might at least have made them aware of the importance of systematic procedures and provided them with a few general rules of conduct, the Prussian foreign service was in a sorry state in 1862—disorganized, undisciplined, and destitute of either uniform method or clear channels of communication.

These conditions were too serious to be corrected overnight; nor were they. A source of immediate concern to Bismarck when he took office, they continued to demand his attention not only during the years in which he was founding the Reich but also in those that followed, when he had to expand the Prussian foreign service to meet the needs of the empire. If, in the end, he succeeded in transforming the chaos of 1862 into order and efficiency, in improving the personnel and the performance of the Foreign Ministry, and in bringing the diplomatic service to a level of technical excellence that was probably unsurpassed in Europe, it was certainly due in part to the critical capacity which had been brought to bear upon Johanna's style in 1847 and which, later, watched over the education of the candidates for the Bismarckian foreign service.[5]

[3] Arthur von Brauer, *Im Dienste Bismarcks: Persönliche Erinnerungen,* edited by Helmuth Rogge (Berlin, 1936), p. 101.

[4] Ludwig Reiners, *Stilkunst: Ein Lehrbuch deutscher Prosa* (4. Aufl., München, 1951), p. 359.

[5] For a fuller discussion of the achievements and the limitations of Bismarck as educator of the foreign service, see Gordon A. Craig, "Bismarck and his Ambassadors: The Problem of Discipline," *Foreign Service Journal,* xxxiii (June 1956), 20 ff.

But it was not only criticism and the other forms of deliberate indoctrination that effected improvement in Prussian diplomacy after 1862. Much was accomplished also by the force of example. Bismarck's great personal triumphs in the 1860's gave a new luster to the diplomatic profession; and the young men who were drawn to it by this fact regarded their chief as the embodiment of all the arts of diplomacy and wanted to learn them from him. Some of them were willing to do the most routine tasks for the mere privilege of observing his methods; and we find Ludwig Raschdau writing: "We [Foreign Ministry] counsellors were perhaps really only hacks, but at least daily observation gave us the advantage of following the master's work regularly."[6] Some came to study in order that they might in time surpass their teacher; and sometimes their eagerness to do the latter made their study imperfect and their understanding incomplete. But few who were associated with him for any length of time went away without feeling that they had been privileged to see political genius at work.

What were the specific qualities that made Bismarck appear, to his own and later generations, to be the very model of diplomacy, and which continue to arouse reluctant admiration even in the breasts of those who disapprove of his methods or the results of his labors? Perhaps, if we seek these out, we can gain some understanding of the reasons for Bismarck's successes in foreign policy and for the failures of his immediate, and some of his more remote, successors. From such an attempt, moreover, we may even come closer to an appreciation of the uses and the limitations of diplomacy itself.

I

Bismarck came to diplomacy late and as an outsider. He was already thirty-six years old, a firmly established landholder, and a Landtag deputy with a budding reputation when he was appointed as Prussian envoy to the federal diet at Frankfurt in 1851. Yet he wasted no time in mastering the rudiments of his new profession. In the first weeks of his mission, he wrote to his wife, who had not yet joined him, "In the art of saying absolutely nothing with lots of

[6] Ludwig Raschdau, *Unter Bismarck und Caprivi* (2. Aufl., Berlin 1939), p. 64.

words I am making raging progress, and I write dispatches of many pages which read just as plain and blunt as any leading article, and if Manteuffel [the Minister President] can say what's in them after he has read them, then he can do more than I."[7]

One has only to read a few of the Frankfurt dispatches to realize that this need not be taken too seriously. The impressive thing is rather the speed with which Bismarck acquired that gift so essential to the diplomat in the field: the ability in a written report to analyze a situation and to disclose which of its features merit special attention. Years later, the novelist Theodor Fontane wrote:

> Bismarck says in one of his letters: "The art of landscape painting does not lie in the ability to reproduce a whole landscape faithfully, but much more in being able to discover the *one* point by which *this* particular landscape is to be distinguished from all others." This is wonderfully true and is not restricted merely to landscapes, but to any given situation.[8]

This ability to discern the salient feature Bismarck possessed from the very beginning; and, despite his attempts at self-depreciation, he also possessed the art of presenting what it revealed to him in a manner that wholly justified the right he exercised later of criticizing the stylistic delinquencies of his subordinates. Manteuffel can have had no trouble in understanding the reports of one who, if he had not been a diplomat, would probably have become one of Germany's greatest letter-writers in any case. Bismarck's dispatches were well organized and written in clear, forceful language; their arguments were systematically marshaled and supported by the skillful use of analogy and citation; and they were enlivened with much concrete detail, with sudden flashes of humor, and with many phrases that are difficult to forget once they have been read. The great dispatch of May 1856 in which Bismarck described Austria and Prussia "ploughing the same disputed acre" and waiting for war "to set the clock of evolution at the right hour" illustrates these qualities,[9] as do the remarkable letters written to Leopold von Gerlach in the following year.[10]

[7] *Briefe an seine Braut und Gattin,* p. 281.

[8] Theodor Fontane, *Briefe an seine Freunde* (2 vols., Berlin, 1925), II, 20.

[9] Otto von Bismarck, *Die gesammelten Werke* (15 vols. in 19, Berlin, 1924 ff.), II, 142.

[10] *Ibid.,* XIV/1, especially 464-474.

To his profession Bismarck brought a not inconsiderable knowledge of Europe and its courts and peoples, and this he eagerly expanded as the years passed and as he moved from Frankfurt to St. Petersburg and from there to Paris. He was always a good linguist, recognizing that languages were the doors that led to an understanding of other lands; and he read and remembered the literary masterpieces of Germany's neighbors. The diversity of his reading is shown in that rather severe letter to Johanna that is quoted above, for Bismarck, before sending it to his fiancée, appended to it some verses of an unnamed French poet, a long poem written by Thomas Chatterton, and the Lord's Prayer in Italian (this last, apparently, because he liked the sound of it).[11] When he moved from the field to the Foreign Ministry in Berlin, Bismarck had much less opportunity than formerly to use the languages he had acquired; and he resorted to all sorts of expedients to keep them alive. In the late 1860's he was still writing stilted but amusing letters in English to the friend of his youth, John Lothrop Motley;[12] in the 1880's he was still carrying on fitful conversations in Russian with his Eastern specialist, Arthur von Brauer, and as late as 1890 he could still exchange pleasantries in that language with a Petersburg correspondent. At all times his marginal comments on Foreign Ministry drafts were written as frequently in Latin, Russian, English, French, or Italian as in his own tongue.[13] The extent to which Bismarck's knowledge of languages other than his own facilitated rapport with representatives of other lands would be difficult to gauge, but it was surely not inconsiderable.

Bismarck always enjoyed travel; and, once he had become a diplomat, he traveled with deliberate purpose. He made this clear in September 1855 when Leopold von Gerlach reproached him for paying a visit to Paris and suggested that one's political principles could only be defiled by contact with that city. Bismarck replied:

[11] *Briefe an seine Braut und Gattin*, pp. 39-41.
[12] *Gesammelte Werke*, xiv/2, especially 762.
[13] Brauer, *Im Dienste Bismarcks*, pp. 97 ff. The journalist, Ignatiew Lwow, who talked with the former Chancellor at Friedrichsruh in April 1890, wrote: "The Prince spoke Russian with me on three different occasions. He expressed regret that he had almost forgotten the Russian language, but said he could still read it because, after the second page, he was carried along by the meaning. Aside from that, he had never learned the language of the Russian

You criticize me for being in Babylon, but you surely cannot demand from a diplomat hungry for knowledge the kind of political chastity that sits so well on a soldier like Lützow or on an independent country gentleman. In my opinion I must learn to know the elements in which I have to move, and I must do so by my own observation as far as opportunities present themselves to me.[14]

Ein lernbegieriger Diplomat! This was a true description of Bismarck during his twelve years in the field, and his whole subsequent career testified to the thoroughness with which he went about the business of accumulating data about the resources, the governmental structure, and the ruling elites of the European states, as well as about their present and potential power, their conception of their own interests and—most important—what they knew and thought about the questions in which Prussia was vitally interested. "I have just come back from London," he wrote to Albrecht von Roon in July 1862. "The people there are much better informed about China and Turkey than about Prussia. Loftus [the British envoy in Berlin] must be writing more nonsense to his minister than I thought."[15] These personal impressions, added to and corrected over the years, gave Bismarck a perspective that could not have been provided merely by reading dispatches, and from his reflections upon them came some of his most striking general observations about the characteristic behavior of the different European states. Some of these have an almost startling relevance to our concerns. When, for instance, the Austrian minister Kálnoky complained about the difficulties that the Russians caused whenever he sought to arrange negotiations with them, Bismarck, drawing on his memory of his own St. Petersburg years, wrote: "This natural defect of the Russians will not be cured in accordance with the rules of Austrian psychiatry. Russia is more an elementary force than a government, more a mastodon than a diplomatic entity, and

---

salon; he had only been acquainted with the literary-journalistic language and above all that of the servants, the coachmen, muzschiks, huntsmen—with the language of the people in which the magic *Nitschewo* plays such a part." *Bismarck Gespräche,* edited by Willy Andreas in collaboration with K. F. Reinking, III (Bremen, 1963), 33 f.

[14] *Gesammelte Werke,* xiv/1, 415.

[15] Albrecht Graf von Roon, *Denkwürdigkeiten* (5. Aufl., 3 vols., Berlin, 1905), II, 101.

she must be treated like bad weather, until things are different."[16]

Before he was called back to Berlin in 1862, to take the post he was to hold for almost thirty years, Bismarck had acquired a knowledge of Europe, great linguistic ability, a mastery of diplomatic forms and procedures, and a capacity for analysis and reporting far beyond the average. Moreover, in St. Petersburg he had learned the difficulties of representation at a court where the ruler prefers to consort with soldiers rather than with diplomats—a circumstance that he was to complain about on many occasions in his later career, but which he accepted as a fact of life.[17] In Frankfurt, earlier, he had also had his first experience in negotiation and, in his dealings with the representatives of the lesser German courts during the Crimean war, had demonstrated a decided flair for it.[18] In short, he understood the principal functions of the working diplomat—representation, reporting, and negotiation—as only a professional can understand them; and this was not unimportant. For, apart from the expertise and the precision that it lent to the statecraft of his Berlin years, what Bismarck had learned in the field gave him a realistic view of the capabilities of diplomatic agencies. He may have made mistakes in the way in which he adjusted relations between the Foreign Ministry and the field—and how serious they were will be treated in a later chapter[19]—but they were never mistakes that stemmed from naïveté or from an overestimation of what the diplomat in the field could be expected to accomplish.

In addition to these professional or technical skills, Bismarck possessed certain qualities of mind and personality which, in his Berlin years, impressed his co-workers and seemed to them to contribute to the success of his statecraft. He was a man of unfailing courtesy and great charm and, on occasion, could be witty and even genial;[20]

---

[16] Brauer, *Im Dienste Bismarcks*, p. 127.

[17] See, for instance, Craig, *Politics of the Prussian Army*, pp. 261-266.

[18] See A. O. Meyer, *Bismarcks Kampf mit Oesterreich am Bundestag zu Frankfurt* (Berlin and Leipzig, 1927), pp. 100-120, 207-249, and Kurt Borries, *Preussen im Krimkrieg* (Stuttgart, 1930), pp. 204 ff.

[19] See below, Chapter Four.

[20] Wit also had its uses. The ambassador and later Imperial Chancellor Hohenlohe wrote in the 1880's: "Bismarck handles everything with a kind of high spirits which gives him a great advantage over the timid minds of the old European diplomacy." Quoted in Ludwig Reiners, *Bismarck* (2 vols., München, 1956-57), I, 25.

and, although he had a good opinion of his own abilities, he was free from the kind of personal vanity that made the Russian Chancellor Gorchakov ludicrous and ruined the career of Harry Arnim, Germany's ambassador to Paris in the early 1870's.[21] He was too good a diplomat to make the mistake of thinking that more than short-run advantages were to be gained by falsehood in direct communications with other powers; and he knew, in any case, that there were other ways of hiding the truth when it was necessary. Therefore, although he was sometimes disingenuous in dealing with his own subordinates,[22] with foreign envoys he generally obeyed that part of the diplomatic code that held that gentlemen do not lie to one another. For all of these reasons, foreign diplomats found that doing business with him was pleasant, and even stimulating, and often came to the point of giving him their full confidence.

Had he been asked to evaluate his own gifts, Bismarck would almost certainly have placed emphasis upon caution and patience. Shortly after he became Minister President, he wrote: "I am now conducting foreign policy in the same way that I used to go on snipe hunts, and I don't put my foot forward until I have tested the hillocks on which I have to step to see whether they are sound and can hold me."[23] He was no believer in action before conditions were favorable, and he continually urged patience on his aides. "We can set our watches," he wrote to his envoy in Munich in February 1869, "but the time passes no more quickly because of that, and the ability to wait while conditions develop is a prerequisite of practical

[21] Bismarck always insisted that statecraft was not a matter of personal vanity, and his objection to Arnim was caused not only by the ambassador's opposition to the policy laid down in Berlin, but by the Chancellor's conviction that he was a "vain, unscrupulous egoist," who put his own prestige above state interest. See Hartung in *Historische Zeitschrift,* CLXXI, 58. For Bismarck's views of Gorchakov, see *Bismarck Gespräche,* III, 35 f.

[22] See below, Chapter Four. By misleading his own envoys, of course, Bismarck was seeking to mislead the courts to which they were accredited, and this can hardly be described as scrupulous honesty. But the whole question of truth in diplomatic intercourse is a difficult one; and it is important not to accept such over-simplified and prejudiced views as that of Holstein, who claimed that Bismarck had "a complete contempt . . . of the truth." See *The Holstein Papers,* edited by Norman Rich and M. H. Fisher, I. *Memoirs and Political Observations* (Cambridge, 1955), p. 119.

[23] A. O. Meyer, *Bismarck, der Mensch und der Staatsmann* (Stuttgart, 1949), p. 117.

policy."[24] In any evolving situation, he felt, it was a mistake to commit oneself to a definite course of policy too soon, and he insisted on this all the more because he knew that this was a weakness to which his fellow countrymen were especially prone. "It was always a failing of the Germans," he said late in life, "to want to attain all or nothing and, in their headstrong way, to rely on one particular course."[25] Indulgence of this proclivity he prevented while he was in power. It was only after his time that it reassumed its influence in German diplomacy.

Bismarck's closest associates in the Foreign Ministry—Bülow the elder, Bucher, Radowitz in the seventies; Hatzfeldt, Brauer, Raschdau in the eighties; and Holstein until he began to have private doubts in the middle eighties[26]—appreciated the above qualities but reserved their greatest admiration for Bismarck's decisiveness, his sureness of touch and his infinite resourcefulness. Bismarck fully believed that there were moments in foreign policy which, as he said in 1866, "never come again"—this was, indeed, why foreign affairs seemed more important to him than domestic politics[27]—and he believed it was the statesman's duty to fasten upon those moments. Despite his preachments of caution, therefore, he could at such times act with a speed, authority, and, if necessary, a brutality that never failed to impress his subordinates. He had, one of them wrote, the quality that Thucydides admired in Themistocles: the ability, by some hidden force of mind or character, to fasten immediately, after short deliberation, upon what was needed in a given situation.[28] His fertility in expedients was rarely found wanting, and his subordinates came to rely upon it to an extent that aroused the amusement of outsiders. "That anyone could help Him in a matter of importance," Maximilian Harden wrote later, "even the

[24] Hajo Holborn, "Bismarck und Werthern," *Archiv für Politik und Geschichte*, v (1925-26), 482.

[25] *Gesammelte Werke*, ix, 49 f.

[26] Holstein's growing doubts about Bismarck's policies are discussed below, Chapter Two. Hatzfeldt's late views are outlined in H. Krausnick, "Botschafter Graf Hatzfeldt und die Aussenpolitik Bismarcks," *Historische Zeitschrift*, CLXVII (1943), 566 ff.

[27] On this, see Hans Rothfels, "Sinn und Grenzen des Primats der Aussenpolitik," *Aussenpolitik*, vi (1955), 277.

[28] Brauer, *Im Dienste Bismarcks*, p. 102.

members of his little club [*Zunftwelt*] would not believe. God gave *Him* the word while he slept."[29]

All of the technical and personal qualities mentioned here played their part in Bismarck's diplomacy. Yet many other men, even in Bismarck's own time, had mastered the professional diplomat's skills, and not a few of them possessed the other gifts listed above. We have not gone very far toward the heart of Bismarck's statecraft if we stop here; nor have we explained why so many people have regarded him as a kind of historical phenomenon that will not recur, a model against which all other statesmen should be measured.

Yet perhaps the answer is not far to seek. In his famous essay on "Politics as a Vocation," Max Weber asks: "What kind of a man must one be if he is to be allowed to put his hand on the wheel of history?"; and he answers his own question by saying: ". . . three pre-eminent qualities are decisive for the politician: passion, a feeling of responsibility, and a sense of proportion."[30] Although he never mentions him in the course of his essay, Weber might just as well have been describing Otto von Bismarck.

II

When I speak here of passion I do not mean the sort of thing one flies into, or the sultry emotion that the Hays Office used to try to keep from the cinema screen, but rather the quality that enables men to escape the fate of the Laodiceans whom Dante found confined in the dark plain of limbo: the quality of wholehearted devotion and total commitment to something. This kind of passion Bismarck possessed in full measure; and the something to which he brought his devotion was his profession: the office he held and the duties he was called upon to perform in the service of his King.

Considering the lack of enthusiasm with which Bismarck approached his profession in the first years, one would never have imagined him capable of a thorough-going commitment of his energies to it. "No one," he wrote to his wife in May 1851, "not even

---

[29] *Die Zukunft*, LXVII (1909), 380.

[30] *From Max Weber: Essays in Sociology*, translated and edited by H. H. Gerth and C. Wright Mills (New York, 1946), p. 115.

the most ill-disposed cynic of a democrat, could believe how much charlatanry and pompousness there is in this diplomacy business;"[31] and a month later he was writing Ludwig von Gerlach that he found in his new occupation none of the zest that he was used to in life on his estate, in parliament, and in his party.[32] But this was a fleeting mood. He was soon captivated by his new work; and his engrossment in it grew with the years and assumed disconcerting forms. Brauer, his Near Eastern specialist in the 1880's, tells us, for instance, that, although he was a frequent visitor in the Bismarck home, it was some time before the Chancellor recognized that his guest was the same person as the man whose memoranda about Turkey and Egypt he read daily but whose face he never looked at.[33] Moreover, this profound absorption was accompanied by an emotional devotion to the task that communicated itself to some observers as an almost demonic force.[34]

It was a devotion to the job that excluded personal vanity and prejudice. This is not, of course, meant to imply that Bismarck as a private person was immune to the baser passions, for he was not. It is well known that in his personal relationships he was often swept by gusts of jealousy and rage, that he could admit to having lain awake all night hating,[35] and that he could permit his personal antipathies to degenerate into vindictiveness and persecution.[36] Yet the very violence of these internal fires makes more impressive the fact that he generally kept them in check while conducting foreign policy. Bülow the elder wrote to his more famous son, the future Chancellor: "Prince Bismarck is in the habit of saying that indignation and rancor are conceptions foreign to diplomacy. The diplomat is neither a preacher of penitence, nor a judge in a criminal court, nor a philosopher. His sole and exclusive concern must be the real and downright interest of his country."[37] Bismarck

[31] *Briefe an seine Braut und Gattin*, p. 281.

[32] *Gesammelte Werke*, xiv/1, 229.

[33] Brauer, *Im Dienste Bismarcks*, pp. 175 f.

[34] *Die Zukunft*, xix (1897), 289 ff.

[35] Erich Eyck, *Bismarck: Leben und Werk* (3 vols., Zurich, 1941-44), iii, 14.

[36] See his letter to Emperor William I concerning Alexander of Battenberg in *The Holstein Papers*, ii. *Diaries* (Cambridge, 1957), pp. 388-393.

[37] Bernhard Fürst von Bülow, *Denkwürdigkeiten* (4 vols., Berlin, 1930-31), iv, 289.

himself in a well-known passage in one of his letters to Leopold von
Gerlach makes the same point with greater force and clarity.

Sympathies and antipathies with respect to foreign Powers and persons
I cannot justify to my sense of duty to the foreign service of my
country, either in myself or in others. Therein lies the embryo of
disloyalty toward one's master or the land one serves. And especially
when one undertakes to arrange one's current diplomatic connections
and the maintenance of friendly relations in peacetime in accordance
with those things, one ceases in my opinion to conduct politics and
begins to act according to personal caprice. In my view, not even the
King has the right to subordinate the interests of the fatherland to
personal feelings of love and hate toward the foreigner. . . .[38]

Otto Vossler is certainly correct in saying that no one can read
this passage, with its emphatic use of terms like "justify," "duty,"
"service," "disloyalty," "caprice," and "right," without being impressed by its moral and ethical earnestness.[39] Certainly it leaves
little doubt that Bismarck's passionate devotion to his office was
animated by something more than the interest and importance of
the work or even the patriotism that he felt as a Prussian officer and
servant of his King. Behind it there was a deep sense of responsibility, which had its roots in Bismarck's religious faith.

Ludwig Bamberger once wrote: "Prince Bismarck believes firmly
and deeply in a God who has the remarkable faculty of always
agreeing with him."[40] That is, perhaps, clever; but it should not be
allowed to throw doubt on the genuineness of Bismarck's faith or its
importance in his statecraft. Bismarck was not ostensibly devout;
the faith that he acquired painfully as a young man he had
always to struggle to maintain, and that he sometimes believed the
struggle was in vain may be shown by the way in which, late in
life, he compared himself to Peter sinking beneath the waves.[41] But
however persistent his internal doubts, he clung to his faith in God's

[38] *Gesammelte Werke*, xiv/1, 465.
[39] Otto Vossler, "Bismarcks Ethos," *Historische Zeitschrift*, CLXXI (1951), 274.
[40] S. von Kardorff, *Wilhelm von Kardorff* (Berlin, 1936), p. 120.
[41] On Bismarck's religious views, see, *inter alia*, Friedrich Meinecke, "Bismarcks Eintritt in den christlich-germanischen Kreis," *Historische Zeitschrift*,
xc (1903), 56 ff.; A. O. Meyer, *Bismarcks Glaube* (4. Aufl., München,
1933), *passim*; Heinrich Ritter von Srbik, *Deutsche Einheit* (4 vols.,
München, 1935-42), III, 66-70; Egmont Zechlin, *Bismarck und die Grundlegung der deutschen Grossmacht* (Stuttgart, 1930), pp. 96 ff; Vossler in *His-*

providence and found personal comfort in the doctrine of justification.[42] And these things helped determine his conception of his
office, supplied him with the strength to accept its burdens, and,
ultimately, gave him confidence to make the decisions his office
forced him to make.

"I am God's soldier," he wrote to Johanna when he first learned
that he was to be sent to Frankfurt, "and where He sends me
there must I go, and I believe that He does send me and that He
shapes my life as He needs it."[43] This has sometimes been taken
merely as an ingratiating plea to a devout wife who did not want to
have to move her family and furniture to another city; and it
might be accepted as such if it stood alone. But it is one of many
statements that show that Bismarck did not regard diplomacy as a
mere job, but as a *vocatio*, an office to which he had been called by
God. "I didn't ask for the royal service," he wrote to Gerlach in
May 1860, "or search for personal honor in it, at least in a pre-
meditated way . . . God set me unexpectedly in it."[44] And if it was
God's will that he do this job, then doing it as well as he could
was both an expression of obedience and an act of service. "I believe that I am obeying God when I serve my King," he said on
one occasion;[45] and, again, "It is precisely my living evangelical and
Christian faith that lays upon me the duty—in behalf of the land
where I was born and for whose service God created me and where
high office has been entrusted to me—to guard that office against all
sides."[46] Here, of course, we hear echoes of Luther's concept of *Beruf*,
or vocation, as the work specifically assigned to God to the individual
so that in performing it he might at one and the same time do his
duty to God and to his fellow men.[47]

---

torische Zeitschrift, CLXXI; and, more recently, Leonhard von Muralt, *Bismarcks Verantwortlichkeit* (Göttingen, 1955), especially pp. 38-140, and Pastor Franz Pahlmann, "Der Stand des Gesprächs über Bismarcks Glauben," *Geschichte in Wissenschaft und Unterricht*, VII (1956), 207-222.

[42] Wilhelm Schüssler, *Um das Geschichtsbild* (Gladbeck, 1953), p. 139; Erich Marcks, *Otto von Bismarck: Ein Lebensbild* (Stuttgart, 1915), p. 250.

[43] *Briefe an seine Braut und Gattin*, p. 269.

[44] *Gesammelte Werke*, XIV/1, 549.

[45] Moritz Busch, *Tagebuchblätter* (Leipzig, 1899), I, 247.

[46] *Gesammelte Werke*, XI, 249.

[47] See Karl Holl, *Gesammelte Aufsätze zur Kirchengeschichte*, I. *Luther* (6. Aufl., Tübingen, 1932), 259 ff., 392, 396.

Bismarck's faith also helped him bear the burdens that went with the authority of his office, especially the heavy weight of decisions that could bring war, and even defeat, upon his country. Despite the undeniable personal satisfaction that he derived from wielding power, he never took its responsibilities lightly or callously; and he was always sensitive to the charge that he was ruthless, without scruple, and without conscience. His job was a lonely one, and in it he had to do things which, by the standard of any religion in the world, were immoral things. "Would to God," he wrote in the famous letter to Andrae-Roman in December 1865, "that I did not have other sins upon my soul besides those the world knows of." But, he continued, far from being ruthless,

> as a statesman I am not ruthless *enough* but rather cowardly in my feelings; and this is so because it isn't always easy in the questions that come to me to win that clarity in whose soil grows confidence in God. Anyone who reproaches me for being a politician without conscience does me injustice and should sometime try out his own conscience on *this* battlefield.[48]

The fact of the matter was that the dirty jobs had to be done, and the man doing them had to continue to hope that God's grace would be extended to him. "If it hadn't been for me," Bismarck said once, "there wouldn't have been three great wars, 80,000 men would not have died and parents, brothers, sisters and widows would not be mourning. But that I have had to settle with God."[49]

The faith that sustained Bismarck in the big questions of life and death quite clearly supported him in the lesser, but nonetheless important, tasks of his office. At the outset of his career as a diplomat he had written to his wife: "I will do my job. Whether God gives me the brains for that purpose is *His* business."[50] A decade later he put the same thought in more elegant language when he said that the God who had made him unexpectedly a diplomat would watch over his actions "as long as I search earnestly for what is for His service in my office, and if I go wrong He will hear my

[48] *Gesammelte Werke*, xiv/2, 709.
[49] Vossler in *Historische Zeitschrift*, clxxi, 286. In this connection, Holl's comments on Luther's recognition of the conflict between *Personalethik* and *Berufsethik* are interesting. *Gesammelte Aufsätze*, i, 282 ff.
[50] *Briefe an seine Braut und Gattin*, p. 271.

daily prayer and change my heart or send me friends who will do so."[51]

It is clear from all this that the decisiveness and sureness of touch so much admired by Bismarck's followers were not merely the products of a dynamic personality or of professional virtuosity, but had other roots; and one can understand more easily now the passion Bismarck brought to his vocation and the confidence with which he performed his duties. Nevertheless, the belief that one is a chosen instrument of God can be, and often has been, a dangerous belief, leading to *hubris* and megalomania. What prevented Bismarck from treading this same path? Here we come to the third of the qualities mentioned by Max Weber: a sense of proportion.

III

In one of the many essays written in Germany about Bismarck since 1945, Franz Schnabel has described the Chancellor as "the last great representative in the line of classical diplomats," "a 'member of the guild' with Choiseul, Kaunitz, Talleyrand and Metternich," and one who believed, like them, that "politics was . . . an exact science concerned with calculable magnitudes."[52] About this claim two things must be said. First, it is dangerous to seek to classify Bismarck, and to make him a Kaunitzian does even more injustice to the character of his statecraft than to describe him—as some writers have done recently—as a Bonapartist.[53] Second, and more important, it is simply not true that Bismarck believed politics to be "an exact science concerned with calculable magnitudes." Otto Pflanze has pointed out how deep an aversion Bismarck had to the rationalistic belief that there were natural laws in society equivalent to those in the structure of the universe and how this affected his view of his own profession. To him politics was always

---

[51] *Gesammelte Werke,* xiv/1, 549.

[52] Franz Schnabel, "The Bismarck Problem," in *German History: Some New German Views,* edited by Hans Kohn (Boston, 1954), pp. 74 f.

[53] See, for instance, H. Gollwitzer, "Das Cäsarismus Napoleons III," *Historische Zeitschrift,* CLXXIII (1952), 30, 65 f.; but compare Gustav Adolf Rein, *Die Revolution in der Politik Bismarcks* (Göttingen, 1957), chap. 3 and especially pp. 127-132.

an art rather than a science;[54] he repeatedly and specifically denied that it was either exact or logical;[55] and, throughout his career, he was conscious of the limitations imposed upon the man who practiced it. If he did not actually say that politics is "the art of the possible,"—late in life he attributed this definition, or one like it, to Pope Pius IX—he certainly believed it;[56] and it was this belief that lent proportion and perspective to his statecraft.

There is no doubt that Bismarck would have accepted the proportion that the first law of politics—and especially of foreign politics —is that one can rarely do exactly what one would like to do. The course that theory would define as the best in a given contingency, circumstances usually render impracticable; and the statesman finds himself compelled to settle for the least harmful of a number of unpleasant alternatives.[57] Bismarck never forgot this, and, from hard experience, he came to know the factors that, in given cases, could, and generally did, limit his freedom of choice and action.

Prussian, and later German, foreign policy was, for one thing, limited in its freedom by the nation's geographical position. This made a vigilant and active foreign policy essential, for, as Bismarck wrote in 1857, "a passive lack of planning, which is content to be left alone, is not for us, situated as we are in the middle of Europe."[58] On the other hand, it forbade adventures in exotic and exciting areas remote from the nation's main sphere of interest, activity, and danger. Thus, Bismarck could say to a colonial enthusiast in the 1880's, "Your map of Africa is very beautiful, but my map of Africa is in Europe. Here is Russia and here is France, and here we are in the middle. That is my map of Africa."[59]

[54] See, for instance, Gesammelte Werke, IX, 399; Otto Pflanze, Bismarck and the Development of Germany: The Period of Unification, 1815-1871 (Princeton, 1963), p. 89.

[55] For instance, in the speech to the delegation from Göttingen University in July 1892. Gesammelte Werke, XIII, 467 ff. See also "Bismarck und Napoleon III. Erinnerungen des Botschafters Hatzfeldt," Berliner Monatshafte, 18. Jahrgang (1940), 501.

[56] See Georg Büchmann, Geflügelte Wörter (Volksausgabe nach der 29. Aufl., Berlin, 1943), p. 379; and, for the attribution, Bismarck Gespräche, III, 95.

[57] Bismarck fully agreed with Machiavelli here. Cf. Gesammelte Werke, XIII, 468 and Il Principe, chap. 21, Discorsi, Book 1, chap. 6.

[58] Gesammelte Werke, XIV/1, 474.

[59] Ibid., VIII, 646.

Germany's policy was limited also by her power at any given moment, and Bismarck's appreciation of this—so dramatically illustrated during the years of the constitutional conflict—need not be elaborated, except to note that—unlike some later statesmen in his own and other countries—he never took too restricted a view of power and always recognized that it included both a nation's actual and potential military and economic strength, and its reputation as well. He knew—if only from studying and taking advantage of British mistakes in Palmerston's last years and in the period from 1866 to 1870[60]—how much a nation's diplomacy depends upon its reliability in the matter of promises and threats; and he guarded Germany's reputation as jealously as he did her military resources.

And there were other limitations that had to be observed. The freedom of Prusso-German diplomacy was always limited by the nature of its international setting. Opportunities like those that were offered to it when the European concert was riven by dissension, as in the years from 1856 to 1870, were not likely to recur in times when there was a consensus among the powers, and a wise statesman had to adjust his policy accordingly. At any given moment, moreover, Germany's freedom to act was limited by the groupings of the powers, the strength and reliability of allies, and other facts of international life. It was equally affected by the nature of its domestic constitutional arrangements; and, while Bismarck did not have to reckon with anything like democratic control of foreign policy, he could never completely ignore public opinion; and even his relative freedom in this respect was balanced by the way in which he was limited, and his policy disrupted, by the prerogatives and prejudices of his sovereign,[61] to say nothing of those forays into politics by military and other irresponsible agencies that were so much a

[60] See Horst Michael, *Bismarck, England und Europa* (München, 1930), *passim; Aus dem Leben Theodor von Bernhardis* (8 vols., Leipzig, 1893-1906), VI, 46; Gordon A. Craig, "Great Britain and the Belgian Railways Dispute," *American Historical Review*, L (1945), 738 ff. and especially 755-760; and Pflanze, *Bismarck and the Development of Germany*, pp. 243 ff., 291, 382.

[61] See any of the numerous accounts of Bismarck's difficulties with the Emperor at the time of the conclusion of the Dual Alliance in 1879. On the question of public opinion, R. J. Sontag finds Bismarck's policy open to criticism precisely because he was persistently indifferent to its wishes when he thought they did not accord with national interest. *Germany and England: Background of Conflict* (New York, 1938), p. 253.

part of the Prusso-German system.[62] Finally, German diplomacy was
limited by the effectiveness of its representatives, who, despite their
schooling at Bismarck's hands, remained subject to human frailties,
and by the nature of the problems with which they, and he, had
to deal—some of which (the problem of Austro-Russian rivalry in
the Balkans, for example) were not susceptible of easy solution,
if, indeed, they were soluble at all.

If Bismarck had refused to recognize any of these limitations—
and he did not—he would still have been held back from *hubris*
by one more that he never forgot. Diplomatic plans, like all human
designs, are always subject to the intervention of chance or providence. The moral of the story of Cesare Borgia, as it is told by
Machiavelli,[63] is that no plan is perfect, that man must always
reckon with the possibility of unforeseeable disaster, and that the
wise man will accept this and not be cowed by it. In this sense at
least, Bismarck was a Machiavellian, recognizing the disruptive po-
tentialities of the unforeseen factors, or, as he called them, the
imponderabilia.

His reflections on this ultimate limitation of diplomacy were influenced, like so much of his political thought, by his religious
beliefs, and specifically by his view of God's providence. To Bismarck
as to Luther, God was a *Deus absconditus* whose will determined
the fate of nations but whose purpose could never be perfectly ap-
prehended by man.[64] The statesman is like a child in a dark room;
he can only hope that God will allow him an occasional glimpse of
light so that he can hobble after it.[65] He dare not anticipate the
ways of providence (it was for this reason that Bismarck, in 1867
and in 1875, steadfastly repudiated the doctrine of preventive
war[66]) and must have the humility to recognize that "by himself he
can create nothing; he can only wait until he hears the step of God
sounding through events and then spring forward and seize the hem

[62] See Fritz Hartung, "Verantwortliche Regierung, Kabinette und Nebenregierungen im konstitutionellen Preussen 1848-1918," *Forschungen zur
brandenburgischen und preussischen Geschichte,* XLIV (1932); and Craig,
Politics of the Prussian Army, chaps. V, VII.

[63] *Il Principe,* chap. 7.

[64] See Holl, *Gesammelte Aufsätze,* I, 51-52.

[65] Meyer, *Bismarcks Glaube,* p. 7.

[66] *Gesammelte Werke,* VIC, 63.

of His garment—that is all."[67] And aside from this—and here was the hardest thing of all to contemplate—the statesman must admit that God may have willed the utter defeat of all his plans and even the destruction of his country. In international politics all of the stories do not have happy endings, and it is God in each case Who writes the final chapters. "As God wills," Bismarck wrote to Roon in January 1864, when Prussian troops were marching toward Jutland. "He will know how long Prussia has to endure. But I would be sorrowful if she should cease to be, God knows."[68] And, twenty-three years later, he said, more sadly: "Nothing in the world is permanent, neither peace treaties nor laws. They come and go; they change; *tempora mutantur, et nos mutamur in illis.* . . . But we do our duty in the present. . . . Whether it lasts is up to God."[69]

IV

Bismarck is generally described in the textbooks as the first *Realpolitiker;* but unfortunately so much has been written about *Realpolitik* that its meaning has become obscure and mixed up with blood and iron and incitement to war by the malicious revision of royal telegrams.[70] This is neither the place nor the time to correct what has become a traditional view. Even so, it may be permissible to suggest that the essence of Bismarck's realism was his recognition of the limitations of his craft, and that it was this, coupled with the passion and the responsibility that he brought to his vocation, that made him a great statesman.

[67] Meyer, *Bismarcks Glaube*, p. 7.
[68] *Gesammelte Werke*, xiv/2, 661.
[69] Quoted by Vossler in *Historische Zeitschrift*, clxxi, 283.
[70] For a sensible discussion, see Hajo Holborn, "Bismarck's *Realpolitik*," *Journal of the History of Ideas*, xxi (1960), especially 94 ff. and notes.

chapter two

THE EPIGONI:

Holstein, Bülow,
Kiderlen-Wächter

IN MAY 1890, three months after Bismarck had been dismissed from office, Paul Kayser, the head of the Colonial Section of the Foreign Ministry, wrote:

> . . . after a quarter of a century of genius, it is a real blessing to be able to be as homely and matter of fact as other governments. Things are decided now in accordance with calculations and argument, and no longer by revelations which do not always emanate from the Holy Spirit. In the great decisive moments of a people's life, genius alone may serve, but in the regular course of affairs it causes confusion and becomes intolerable.[1]

Coming as it did from one who was brought into the Foreign Ministry by Bismarck and shown great kindness and given unusual preferment by him, this statement was singularly free from any regret over the Chancellor's passing. Like many similar statements made in 1890, it was an expression of the satisfaction mediocrity experiences when it is freed from the necessity of competing with superior intelligence. But, apart from this, Kayser's words are interesting because he seems to have assumed that the future course of

---

[1] Walther Frank, "Der geheime Rat Paul Kayser," *Historische Zeitschrift,* CLXVIII (1943), 320.

events was going to be so placid that something far short of genius would be enough for the necessary tasks of statecraft.

This was a false assumption, for, in fact, the period that began in 1890 was not quiet, but was filled with a series of dangerous crises, all of which seem, in retrospect, to have been "decisive moments" in Germany's life, until that fateful day in the autumn of 1914 when the ultimate disaster engulfed her. And, as crisis followed crisis, Kayser's words became increasingly hollow, for German statecraft did not prove adequate to the problems confronting it, and the need for something like genius became ever more painfully evident.

That skeptical observer of the German political scene, Count Monts, once wrote of the Wilhelmine period that, compared with the age that preceded it, it was an age of Epigoni.[2] The Epigoni, it will be remembered, were the sons of the seven heroes who fought against Thebes, and the name has been given also to the followers of Alexander. In both cases, they proved to be inferior to their predecessors, in spirit and accomplishment.

The most important of the men who had to deal with foreign policy in the reign of William II—Baron Friedrich von Holstein, Prince Bülow, and Alfred von Kiderlen-Wächter—were Epigoni in this dual sense. Each of them, by association or reputation, stood in a relationship to Bismarck that was not wholly unlike that of a son to a father. Holstein had served with Bismarck even before the latter was Minister President of Prussia; he had enjoyed the Chancellor's protection in his early years, had been taken into Bismarck's family circle, and had finally been his subordinate in the Foreign Ministry for fourteen years. Bülow was the son of Bismarck's most trusted State Secretary for Foreign Affairs; he had served in numerous posts in the Bismarckian diplomatic service; and he boasted of having studied the great Chancellor's works and profited from them.[3] Alfred von Kiderlen-Wächter was known as the "Swabian Bismarck"[4] and seems to have fancied the appellation and to have

[2] A. Graf von Monts, *Erinnerungen und Gedanken,* edited by K. Nowak and F. Thimme (Berlin, 1932), pp. 287 f.

[3] In his memoirs, Bülow says that Treitschke's *German History* and Bismarck's speeches were the foundation of his political thought. *Denkwürdigkeiten,* IV, 460.

[4] Ernst Jäckh, *Kiderlen-Wächter: Der Staatsmann und der Mensch* (2 vols., Berlin and Leipzig, 1925), I, 34.

sought to impress on others his similarity to the founder of the Reich,[5] going so far, indeed, as to imitate his handwriting.

But, if these three statesmen were Epigoni in the sense of being followers and, at times, imitators of Bismarck, they were Epigoni also in their failure to match their great predecessor's achievement or even to protect his legacy. Each of them departed, in one or more ways, from the principles that guided Bismarck's statecraft, to the detriment of the nation. Each of them lacked, to a striking degree, gifts that had made Bismarck a master of his craft. Indeed—if it is permissible to refer again to Max Weber's formulation of the three pre-eminent qualities that are decisive in the statesman—it may be suggested that each of these Wilhelmine statesmen had a marked deficiency in one of them. Holstein lacked a sense of proportion; Bülow lacked a sense of responsibility; and, if Kiderlen was a passionate man, his passion was not of the kind that animates and inspires statescraft.

I

For fifteen years after Bismarck's fall, Friedrich von Holstein, despite his relatively obscure position of Senior Counsellor in the Political Division of the Foreign Ministry, had more influence in the determination of Germany's foreign policy than anyone except the Emperor himself and his Chancellors; and the first three post-Bismarckian Chancellors followed his advice to a remarkable degree. Neither Caprivi nor his State Secretary for Foreign Affairs, Marschall, had had any previous experience in foreign affairs, and they were utterly dependent upon Holstein's advice. This was generally true also of Prince Chlodwig zu Hohenlohe-Schillingsfürst, who became Chancellor in 1894. Hohenlohe, a gifted but never very self-reliant character (someone once said of him that his motto should be: "I may be weak, but at least I'm not a scoundrel"),[6] had been on intimate terms with Holstein since the early 1870's, had taken

[5] See, for instance, Oscar Freiherr von der Lancken Wackenitz, *Meine dreissig Dienstjahre* (Berlin, 1931), p. 103.

[6] The remark was Werthern's (see Holborn in *Archiv für Politik und Geschichte*, v, 474); his source, *Der Freischütz*, act 3, finale. Hohenlohe's sister Elise once said that her brother made a virtue of meekness, and that it was the basis of all his success. Bülow, *Denkwürdigkeiten*, IV, 463.

his advice with respect to policy and personnel matters during
his mission in Paris and his term as Governor of Alsace-Lorraine,
and, despite occasional flashes of independence, continued to depend
on him during his chancellorship.[7] As for Bülow, he always honored
Holstein as one who had been a friend of his father and who
had been his own mentor during his early years; and he too came
to lean so heavily on him that he continued to consult him even
after Holstein's dismissal in 1906.[8]

Holstein possessed all the obvious qualities to justify the confidence placed in him by Bismarck's first three successors. His experience in foreign affairs was varied and, in terms of time, extensive,
for his career had started back in the days of Bismarck's St.
Petersburg mission. In 1861, indeed, Bismarck, then minister to the
court of Alexander II, had presented the fledgling attaché Holstein
to old Prince Nesselrode, with the words "Here is a diplomat of
the future." The relic of the Vienna Congress answered, "In the
future there will be no diplomacy and no diplomats!"[9]

Holstein refused to be discouraged by this rejoinder, taking it for
what it probably was, an expression of the self-conceit of extreme
age, rather than a prophecy affecting his own future. He persisted
in his chosen career and, between 1862 and 1876, served on a
variety of special missions and in a number of widely separated
posts. In 1864, during the war in Jutland, he was attached to Prussian army headquarters (where the superannuated and irascible
Field Marshal von Wrangel, who did not like diplomats, granted
him the privilege of visiting the front lines, privately expressing
the hope that a Danish sniper might relieve him of future duties

[7] How heavy this dependence was in the period before the chancellorship
has recently been illustrated in Helmuth Rogge, *Holstein und Hohenlohe:
Neue Beiträge zu Friedrich von Holsteins Tätigkeit als Mitarbeiter Bismarcks
und als Ratgeber Hohenlohes, 1874-1894* (Stuttgart, 1957). Holstein's relations with Hohenlohe during the latter's chancellorship are made clear in
Hohenlohe's *Denkwürdigkeiten der Reichskanzlerzeit,* edited by K. A. von
Müller (Stuttgart, 1931).
[8] Holstein was also, until his death, an informal adviser of Kiderlen-Wächter.
Holstein Papers, I, 197.
[9] Holstein himself gave the correct version of this often told story in an
open letter to Harden. *Die Zukunft,* LVI (1906), 229 ff. On Holstein's
diplomatic *début,* see also Kurd von Schlözer, *Petersburger Briefe,* edited by
Leopold von Schlözer (Stuttgart, 1921), pp. 187 ff.

of hospitality); and in 1870, during the French war, he was sent to Florence, apparently to investigate means of sabotaging any Italian plans that might be made to give material assistance to Napoleon III. His most important diplomatic posts were Rio de Janeiro, London, Washington, and Paris, in two of which he had experiences that may have colored the rest of his life. In Washington, he seems to have become so attentive to the wife of U. S. Senator Charles Sumner, the Chairman of the Senate Foreign Relations Committee, that his government had to transfer him;[10] while in Paris he was involved in the difficulties that led to the dismissal and state trial of his chief, Count Harry Arnim. It was widely believed in diplomatic circles that Bismarck had used Holstein as an agent to trap the ambitious ambassador.[11] However that may be, in 1876, the Chancellor, who had had a good opinion of him from the earliest days,[12] brought him back to Berlin and gave him one of the highly coveted positions in the Political Division of the Foreign Ministry, that exclusive inner circle that was the real heart of Bismarck's Foreign Ministry and was referred to by its inmates simply as "A" and, by the less fortunate officials outside the pale, as "The Guards."[13]

Holstein soon proved to be the mainstay of that department. He was already proficient in the necessary technical skills and was a superb drafting officer. Harden said of him years later that he had "learned how to write from Bismarck: clearly, powerfully, and hellishly personally."[14] He mastered the department's files with incredible speed and apparently never forgot anything he read; and he early developed the habit of supplementing the information that

[10] See *Holstein Papers*, I, chaps. 1-4; and, on the affair in Washington, George W. F. Hallgarten, "Fritz von Holsteins Geheimnis," *Historische Zeitschrift*, CLXXVII (1954), 75-83.

[11] See E. von Wertheimer, "Der Prozess Arnim," *Preussische Jahrbücher*, CCXXII (1930), 117 ff.; Hartung in *Historische Zeitschrift*, CLXXI, 48 ff.; Norman Rich, "Holstein and the Arnim Affair," *Journal of Modern History*, XXVIII (1956), 35-54; Rogge, *Holstein und Hohenlohe*, pp. 56 ff., 76.

[12] See, for instance, Bismarck's letter of 26/14 March 1861 to his sister, mentioning his new attaché, Holstein. *Gesammelte Werke*, XIV/1, 568.

[13] On the Political Division, see especially Brauer, *Im Dienste Bismarcks*, pp. 94 ff.; J. M. von Radowitz, *Aufzeichnungen und Erinnerungen*, edited by Hajo Holborn (2 vols., Stuttgart, 1925), I, 255 ff.; Ludwig Raschdau, *Wie ich Diplomat wurde* (Berlin, 1938), p. 43.

[14] *Die Zukunft*, LXVII (1909), p. 387.

could be acquired from the files and the daily dispatches from the
field with a very extensive personal correspondence with ambassadors
and ministers at foreign courts.[15] As the years passed, this knowledge
of the policies and interests of the great powers was extended and
matured, much as Bismarck's had been; and this formidable body
of experience was one of the things that justified the trust that
Bismarck's successors put in his advice. The grouping of the powers
at any moment and the internal situation of Germany's neighbors
Holstein always had at his finger-tips; and the knowledge made him
indispensable to Caprivi, Hohenlohe and Bülow.

To the majority of historians who have written about him Holstein has not seemed an attractive person; and it is doubtful that
the recent and continuing publication of new Holstein papers is
going to change their opinions subtantially.[16] It is perhaps only fair,
therefore, to insist upon Holstein's undeniably good qualities, before
going on to his deficiencies. Arthur von Brauer once wrote of him
that he "possessed in a high degree what Bismarck called 'political
blood.' "[17] He lived, breathed, ate, and drank politics; he wanted nothing else in life than to sit in his office and work; and in the
Political Division he was always the first to arrive in the morning
and the last to leave at night. Moreover, this passionate dedication
to his work was rooted in an equally intense patriotism and in a
deeply felt sense of responsibility to his country.

"He loved Prussia and the German Reich," Harden wrote after
his death, "like a mother and like a bride. He was ready to sacrifice
everything for the fatherland."[18] When he felt the safety of the nation endangered, he reacted strongly and was no respecter of persons. In the middle 1880's, convinced that Bismarck's policies were

[15] *Holstein Papers*, II, xi.
[16] See "Records of Modern Germany," *Times Literary Supplement*, 10
June 1955, pp. 309-310.
[17] Brauer, *Im Dienste Bismarcks*, p. 107.
[18] *Die Zukunft*, LXVII (1909), 418. See also Baroness Spitzemberg's
comment after Holstein's dismissal, when it was being said that he had enough
secret knowledge to destroy the Emperor and the state. "This kind of old
Prussian official could never do that," she wrote. "It would break his heart."
And again: "Despite his ugly human characteristics, he is an absolutely reliable
public servant and a most outstanding man." *Das Tagebuch der Baronin
Spitzemberg: Aufzeichnungen aus der Hofgesellschaft des Hohenzollernreiches*,
edited by Rudolf Vierhaus (Göttingen, 1960), p. 459.

threatening the future of his country, he sought in his own way to combat them. In the years after 1890, when he believed that the powers of the Emperor and the pervasive influence of military agencies were drawing the Empire into dangerous ways, he did everything he could to attack the evil at its root. As early as 1890, he was urging the Kaiser's favorite, Eulenburg, "to take a stand against the idea that military men are more reliable than civilians" and to intimate to his royal master that Waldersee, the Chief of the General Staff and the most politically ambitious of the soldiers, should be dismissed.[19] Later, when the experience of the Krüger telegram seemed to show that the Emperor was incorrigible, he urged the Chancellor to resign unless William gave up his private and irresponsible conversations with diplomats and soldiers.[20] Holstein's persistence in urging such restraints fully justifies Hutten-Czapski's tribute to him for having seen the crucial flaw in the administration of foreign relations under William II and for having tried to do something to remove it.[21]

Yet these good qualities were marred by grave fundamental defects, the first of which was an intensely personal view of life and politics, which pervaded all aspects of his diplomacy.

Perhaps the sternest judgment ever made of Holstein was that written by Lothar von Schweinitz, the long-term ambassador in St. Petersburg, who said of Holstein, whom he had known as early as 1864, "he has a malicious character and allows himself to be influenced by personal antipathies. . . . One cannot deny that he has outstanding intelligence, but he has the spirit and character of a hunchback."[22] Schweinitz and Holstein were old adversaries;[23] but even Holstein's friends admitted that he was plagued by an ineradicable distrust of his fellow men and regarded everyone with whom he came into professional contact as either a scoundrel or an

[19] Fritz Haller, *Philipp Eulenburg, the Kaiser's Friend* (2 vols., London, 1930), I, 129, 306. See also Friedrich Haselmayr, *Ein Jahrzehnt wechselvoller kaiserlicher Politik, 1890-99* (München, 1962), pp. 246, 273.

[20] Hohenlohe, *Reichskanzlerzeit*, pp. 191 f., 309. See also Otto Hammann, *Bilder aus der letzten Kaiserzeit* (Berlin, 1922), p. 17.

[21] Bogdan Graf Hutten-Czapski, *Sechzig Jahre Politik und Gesellschaft* (2 vols., Berlin, 1935-36), I, 557 ff.

[22] H. L. von Schweinitz, *Denkwürdigkeiten*, edited by W. von Schweinitz (2 vols., Berlin, 1927), II, 349.

[23] Rogge, *Holstein und Hohenlohe*, pp. 46, 102.

intriguer, until he was convinced by unquestionable proof that this
was not true.[24] Repeatedly, in letters to Eulenburg and Hohenlohe
about third persons, Holstein's remarks were impregnated with a
hatred that one might expect from a jealous woman but hardly
from a serious statesman;[25] and anyone who reads the incredible and
easily disproved statements that he makes in his memoirs about his
bête noire, the Counsellor and later Ambassador Radowitz, will be
inclined to agree with Wilhelm Schüssler, who has said that the very
fact that Holstein could put this sort of thing down on paper, even
if he did not intend to publish it, speaks against him as a man and
adds substance to the charges made against him by his fellow
diplomats after 1890.[26]

As they were walking by the Foreign Ministry building on the
Wilhelmstrasse one day, Kurd von Schlözer said to Maximilian
Harden:

> There he sits! He has concocted the most indigestible soup for us. In
> every capital he has his agents and spies. Their dispatches provide the
> material for the secret reports from which the Emperor is supposed to
> learn what his envoys are doing. . . . And on testimony of this
> caliber-people like us are hunted out of the service like a maid in
> waiting caught stealing![27]

This wild mixture of metaphor may be forgiven in a man who
had, in fact, been driven from his post at the Vatican by Holstein,
who had disliked him ever since they served in St. Petersburg
together.[28] And Schlözer was not alone. It was widely believed that
Holstein was responsible for the removal of other Bismarckian envoys from their posts in the years following the fall of the great
Chancellor: Radowitz from Constantinople, Werder from St. Peters-

[24] Brauer, *Im Dienste Bismarcks,* p. 107.
[25] See Hammann, *Bilder,* p. 15; and Rogge, *Holstein und Hohenlohe,* pp.
46 f., 183, 185, 240.
[26] Wilhelm Schüssler in *Das historisch-politische Buch,* v (1957), 131;
Holstein Papers, I, *passim,* but especially 91-101; and Hans Goldschmidt,
"Mitarbeiter Bismarcks im aussenpolitischen Kampf," *Preussische Jahrbücher,*
ccxxxvi (1934), 27 ff.
[27] *Die Zukunft,* LVI (1906), 238 f.
[28] *Holstein Papers,* I, 6, 14-16, 64, 68-69; II, 45. Kurd von Schlözer, *Letzte
römische Briefe,* edited by Leopold von Schlözer (Stuttgart, 1924), pp.
183 ff. *Das Tagebuch der Baronin Spitzemberg,* pp. 318 f.

burg, Reuss from Vienna.[29] Even if we admit that there is an element of exaggeration in the stories that circulated about Holstein's personal vendettas, there is more than enough evidence to substantiate Schweinitz's charge that he allowed his conduct of foreign affairs to be influenced by his personal likes and dislikes.

Nor was it only individuals that he judged in this way. His attitude to the great powers of Europe was also affected by his personal prejudices, and here he quite clearly violated that cardinal precept of Bismarckian statecraft which held that to follow one's private sympathies and antipathies with respect to foreign powers was to be derelict in one's duty as a statesman and disloyal to the interests of one's country. Holstein's bitter prejudice against Russia colored the policy he professed, not only in 1890, when the fateful break with St. Petersburg was effected, but even in the 1880's, when Bismarck was still in power. It was so strong that Holstein was incapable of understanding Bismarck's insistence upon retaining the Russian tie; he convinced himself that the Chancellor must have lost his powers of judgment or fallen under the influence of his son Herbert, who, Holstein believed, had been "completely taken in by the Russians."[30] And this conviction led him to attempt to counteract what he considered to be a mistaken policy, by entering into secret relations with the Austrian embassy in Berlin and by using this channel of communication to strengthen the anti-Russian feelings of Germany's chief ally. It has been suggested above that Holstein was driven to this course by patriotic motives, but this hardly justifies a procedure that was used to contradict the very essence of Bismarck's policy, by intimating to the Austrians that the restrictions of the Dual Alliance of 1879 were not real and that Germany would always support Austria in a war with Russia, even if that war was of Austria's choosing.[31]

This course of action was so drastic that it cannot be accounted for merely by Holstein's intense subjectivity in political matters or even by his personal dislike of Russia. It had a more fundamental

[29] *Die Zukunft*, LV (1906), 462 f.

[30] *Holstein Papers*, II, 256, 266, 276, 332. Holstein's aversion to the Russians is discussed in Brauer, *Im Dienste Bismarcks*, p. 421, and especially in H. Krausnick, *Holsteins Geheimpolitik in der Aera Bismarck, 1886-1890* (2. Aufl., Hamburg, 1942), pp. 13-15.

[31] See especially Krausnick, *Holsteins Geheimpolitik*, pp. 35 ff., 58 ff., 71.

cause: namely, Holstein's lack of anything like Bismarck's sense of proportion in foreign affairs.

Because Bismarck recognized the limitations of diplomacy and the possible disruption of human calculations by imponderable factors and acts of God, he was unwilling to commit himself, unless it was absolutely necessary, to a defined course of action for a contingency that had not yet arisen. He preferred a high degree of ambiguity in the international situation, and the very nature of his treaty system, with its complications and apparent inconsistencies, showed this. There was such a thing, Bismarck felt, as overdefining questions and being too anxious to clarify matters, for these practices led to rigidity, and in rigidity lay danger.

Holstein had, and could have, no sympathy with this kind of thinking. His whole being cried out against the idea that man's designs could be overthrown by *imponderabilia*; he felt that these could be foreseen by proper vigilance and devotion to one's task; and he sought to display these qualities himself by rarely leaving his desk and to inculcate them in his diplomats by bombarding them with nervous telegrams,[32] interrupting their leaves,[33] and discouraging them from indulging in distractions like marriage.[34] More important, he felt that the possibility of disruption by unforeseen factors could be reduced, if not eliminated, by simplifying and clarifying Germany's commitments, and by removing the ambiguities and inconsistencies in any political situation in which she was involved.

Holstein, indeed, insisted on making what Bismarck had called the characteristic mistake of the Germans—that of prejudging events and deciding too soon on a given course of action. As Krausnick has written, his severely analytical and logical mind made it impossible for him to see Bismarck's alliance system as a whole or to appreciate the freedom of action and the measure of control it afforded. He saw only its inherent inconsistencies and wished to remove them.[35] When Bismarck's dismissal gave him an opportunity to press for simplifica-

---

[32] See Jäckh, *Kiderlen-Wächter*, I, 177.

[33] Hohenlohe's wife disliked Holstein intensely because, in the days when her husband was in the foreign service, Holstein was always interrupting his leaves of absence and urging him to return to his post for one reason or another. Rogge, *Holstein und Hohenlohe*, p. 234.

[34] Brauer, *Im Dienste Bismarcks*, p. 111.

[35] Krausnick, *Holsteins Geheimpolitik*, p. 80; *Holstein Papers*, I, 127; II, 332.

tion, he did so, and, by doing so, inaugurated—or helped to inaugurate—the fateful division of Europe into two armed camps.

But Holstein's desire for simplification took a still more radical form, which illustrates his lack of the kind of proportion Bismarck possessed. Unlike the great Chancellor, he was not disinclined to anticipate the will of God and to consider preventive war as a means of removing the international ambiguities that offended his tidy soul. In January 1887, the Austrian ambassador in Berlin reported to his government that Holstein had said that "as far as he was concerned he was unmistakably of the opinion that it would be more advantageous, in both the military and the political sense, for Germany to choose the time to anticipate French attacks which were coming in any case sooner or later." Later in the same year, he was in full accord with those German soldiers, like Waldersee, who wanted to precipitate hostilities against Russia, and he bitterly resented the fact that Bismarck made this impossible.[36] Eighteen years later, at a time when Germany's international position had deteriorated and the Franco-Russian and the Anglo-French combinations had come into being, Holstein seems once more to have wished to simplify Germany's problems by means of preventive war. Neither the Emperor nor the Chancellor, Prince Bülow, was entirely clear about the object of the policy that Holstein persuaded them to follow during the Moroccan crisis of 1905; but the testimony of men who discussed the affair with Holstein in later years, and that of subordinates of the Chief of the General Staff, Schlieffen, who was in close contact with Holstein at the time, makes it highly probable that he was bent on forcing war upon France. He was cheated of his desire by the Emperor's precipitate withdrawal from the brink to which he had been led; and he lost his post in consequence. At the end of March 1906 his official career was finished, and he was writing bitterly to Bülow: "H. M. finds me uncomfortable and wants now to make foreign policy directly, without any opposition from the green table. On that account he is using Morocco as an excuse to get rid of me."[37]

---

[36] Krausnick, *Holsteins Geheimpolitik*, pp. 117, 155 ff., 161. For the political activities of the soldiers in 1887, see Craig, *Politics of the Prussian Army*, pp. 268-270.

[37] *Holstein Papers*, IV, no. 950. See also Peter Rassow, "Schlieffen und Holstein," *Historische Zeitschrift*, CLXXIII (1952); Lancken, *Dienstjahre*, pp. 54-55; Monts, *Erinnerungen*, pp. 191-192; *Das Tagebuch der Baronin*

"Germany's international policy was never worse," Harden once
wrote, "and its results never poorer than in the three *lustra* of
Holstein's dominance. . . . When Bismarck departed, France was
isolated; when Holstein went, Germany was."[38] However true this
summary of Germany's changed fortunes, it is hardly fair to Holstein. He never dominated German policy—indeed, he could not do
so in a country in which so many irresponsible agencies intervened
in foreign affairs. As he said himself, he had had nothing to do
with the Krüger telegram, the launching of the Baghdad railway
scheme, the anti-English tirades of the Emperor and the parliamen-
tarians, and other things that weakened Germany's position.[39]

Spitzemberg, pp. 451-52, 453-54. Gerhard Ritter, in *Der Schlieffenplan:
Kritik eines Mythos* (München, 1956), pp. 102-138, argues vigorously against
the thesis presented above. His pages on Schlieffen demonstrate the weakness
of some of the evidence, but they do not explain away that of Wilhelm
Groener, a General Staff officer and a follower of Schlieffen, who during the
crisis and for the rest of his life believed that the Chief of Staff desired war
in 1905. [See Wilhelm Groener, *Lebenserinnerungen*, edited by F. Freiherr
Hiller von Gaertringen (Göttingen, 1957), pp. 83 ff. and, for evidence of a
preventive war psychology in the upper reaches of the army, Generaloberst
von Einem, *Erinnerungen eines Soldaten, 1853-1933* (Leipzig, 1933), pp.
111-114, and *Documents Diplomatiques Francais, 2ième series*, VI, no. 369.] It
is interesting to note that, in two rather ambiguous passages in the introduction to his edition of Schlieffen's letters, Eberhard Kessel, while denying that
Schlieffen's war plan of 1905 had a "preventive war character," suggests that
the Chief of Staff was in fact thinking personally in terms of preventive war
during the Moroccan crisis and says plainly that Schlieffen was as anxious to
come to grips with France in 1905 as he had been in 1867. Generalfeldmarschall Graf Alfred Schlieffen, *Briefe* (Göttingen, 1958), pp. 13 f., 53 f.,
205, 207, 208. As for Holstein, Ritter points out (pp. 126, 134) that there is
no evidence in his dispatches or memoranda that he wanted war in 1905-06.
This is not surprising; but it is hardly conclusive, especially when one remem-
bers that Holstein's desire for preventive war in 1887 (which Ritter does not
mention) is not documented by papers from his own hand either. Ritter's
argument seems to assume that Holstein's and Bülow's intentions were identi-
cal in 1905-06. That so intelligent a person as Holstein would be as willing
as Bülow was to base his policy on a bluff that might be called seems ques-
tionable. See Craig, *Politics of the Prussian Army*, pp. 283 ff. The Holstein
correspondence does not throw a very clear light on Holstein's policy beyond
indicating that he wished to go further than the Emperor or Bülow. See, for
instance, *Holstein Papers*, IV, no. 919.

[38] *Die Zukunft*, LV (1906), 466.
[39] *Ibid.*, LVI (1906), 232 f.

Nevertheless, when this qualification has been made, the fact remains that Holstein's influence in foreign affairs was, at critical moments (at the time of the discussions over the possible renewal of the Reinsurance Treaty, for example, and during the Moroccan affair), very great. It was precisely at those moments that his intense subjectivity, and that fundamental lack of proportion that expressed itself in a hatred of ambiguity so great that it was willing to risk all to remove it, came into play and did irreparable harm to the nation he loved so deeply.

II

In one of the brilliant essays on the disintegration of values that form part of his novel *The Sleep Walkers,* Hermann Broch says that "style is something which uniformly permeates all the living expressions of an epoch."[40] If this is true, Holstein, with his antique Prussian sobriety and simplicity, is hardly to be considered a characteristic figure of the Wilhelmine period.[41] For the style of this period —and here such markedly different observers as Theodor Fontane, Alfred Döblin, and Gustav Stresemann not only agree but use the same words in agreeing—was one of garish display and vulgar ostentation, of byzantine imitation and pretentious theatricality, of cheapness, and superficiality, and spiritual poverty.[42] Of this style, the living expression was not Holstein, but Bülow.

One sees this, of course, in the four massive volumes of memoirs that Bülow left behind him when he died. This staggering work is marked in every page by the inflated and ornate phrase, by a blend of sentimentality and eroticism, especially marked in the author's descriptions of his youthful love affairs, by the constant use of classical quotations (often wholly inappropriate) for purposes of adornment rather than illumination, and by the general superficiality, if not banality, of the author's reflections on general sub-

[40] Part III, chap. 24.
[41] He did speculate on the Bourse and was accused of doing so on the strength of official information that came to him. Perhaps this makes him more typical of an age of materialism than I have said.
[42] See Rudolf Olden, *Stresemann* (Berlin, 1929), pp. 248 ff.; A. Döblin, "Republik," *Die neue Rundschau* (1920/1), p. 78; Theodor Fontane, *Briefe an Friedländer* (Berlin, 1954), p. 305.

jects.[43] And what one sees in Bülow the man of letters, one sees also in Bülow the statesman, for here too he mirrored the characteristics of his age.

No chancellor, except Bismarck, had as varied and thorough a training in foreign affairs as Bernhard von Bülow. The son of one of Bismarck's state secretaries for foreign affairs, he entered the diplomatic service in 1873 and, in the next fifteen years, served in a whole series of pleasant and important posts, including Rome, St. Petersburg, Athens, Vienna, and Paris. In 1878 he was secretary at the Congress of Berlin, the most impressive diplomatic *omnium gatherum* between Vienna and Versailles. From 1888 until 1893 he was minister to Bucharest and, from 1893 to 1897, ambassador in Rome. In the latter year he returned to Berlin to take up the duties of State Secretary, and this post proved to be the stepping stone to the imperial chancellorship, which he assumed in 1900. It was an impressive apprenticeship for a man who would have so many grave international issues to deal with; but it seeems to have taught Bülow only the gestures of statecraft and not its substance.

Statecraft was, to be quite clear about this, a matter of theatrics with Bülow. During his chancellorship, for instance, whenever he had to address the Reichstag on the foreign situation, his speech was prepared long in advance with the aid of Foreign Ministry experts and was sometimes written in large part by the gifted head of the Press Section, Otto Hammann. Bülow then took it off to his estate at Norderney, where he worked over it, and memorized it, and practiced gestures to go with it, and made provision for interruptions, and thought up clever replies to make in case there *were* interruptions. When all this was done, a dress rehearsal was held in the Foreign Ministry, in the presence of Hammann and others, and every movement of the hand and head, every intonation of the voice

---

[43] On the memoirs in general, see F. Freiherr Hiller von Gaertringen, *Fürst Bülows Denkwürdigkeiten: Untersuchungen zu ihrer Entstehungsgeschichte und ihrer Kritik* (Tübingen, 1956). On Bülow's style, see Reiners, *Stilkunst,* pp. 197 f., 569 f.; and the chapters by R. C. Muschler and Eugen Fischer in *Front wider Bülow,* edited by F. Thimme (München, 1931), pp. 366 ff., 390.

was scrutinized and considered from the standpoint of its potential effectiveness on an audience.[44] All of this, of course, necessitated a considerable amount of time and labor; but the point to be noted is that Bülow's time and labor were lavished not on the substance of the speech but on the manner in which it would be delivered. He was an actor performing a role, and the theatrical nature of this occupation meant that he was always somewhat removed from the realities with which he was supposed to be dealing.

This applies with telling force to his diplomacy. No one can contemplate the artful posturing of his Baghdad policy ("With a bow to the British lion and a curtsey to the Russian bear, we will worm our way little by little down to the Persian Gulf!"),[45] the bombast and fustian of the naval and colonial policies, and the elaborately contrived descent of the Emperor upon Tangier in 1905 without concluding that international politics was to Bülow a continual dramatic performance in which he played the leading role. When reality threatened to come stalking in from the wings, however, as it did in the Moroccan affair, he hastily struck the machinery, cancelled the performance, and dismissed the rest of the cast—an experience which Holstein, among others, had to undergo.

The realities were always present, and they were serious enough to engage the attention of any German statesman. The apparent stability of the Franco-Russian alliance, the possibility that British isolation would not be permanent but would be transformed into adherence to one or the other bloc of great powers, the unreliability of Italy as an ally, and the tendency of Austria-Hungary to read more into the terms of the Dual Alliance than was actually there were all matters that had a vital bearing upon Germany's future security. In addition, perhaps the most serious of the real problems, because it affected all the others, was that presented by the character of Germany's ruler, that personally attractive, highly gifted, deplorably energetic sovereign, of whom Alfred Kerr wrote:[46]

[44] A. Zimmermann in *Front wider Bülow*, pp. 223 f. See also E. Jäckh, *ibid.*, pp. 58 f.

[45] G.P., XVII, 375.

[46] Alfred Kerr, "ER" in *Caprichos: Strophen des Nebenstroms* (Berlin, 1926).

*Was man klar an ihm erkannt
War der Mangel an Verstand.
Sonst besass er alle Kräfte
Für die Leitung der Geschäfte.**

William's sallies into politics, his speeches, his communications to foreign envoys and his habit of indulging his own whims and enthusiasms complicated every aspect of German politics; and, as Holstein had warned two Chancellors before Bülow, the efficient handling of other problems depended on the solution of this one.

But Bülow was not a man to grapple seriously with problems. His principle of action—announced in 1903 when he was warned from London that the possibility of Great Britain forming diplomatic ties with the Franco-Russian combination was not entirely unlikely—was expressed in the words *"Wir können die Dinge* meo voto *gar nicht pomadig genug nehmen."*[47] It is not easy to translate this characteristically Bülow-an statement. It means essentially, "About such remote possibilities we need not worry. We cannot take these things too calmly"; but the word *pomadig* is derived from pomade, a greasy substance, and this fact reminds us that Bülow was sometimes known as "the eel," a creature which, if not in fact greasy, goes about its business in a slippery fashion, touching the obstacles it encounters, but slithering by them or undulating around them, presumably retaining serenity of mind as it does so. This is precisely the way Bülow approached the problems that arose during his chancellorship. He touched but did not move them, adjusting himself to their unyielding surfaces, and undulated by, calmly, happily, *pomadig.*

To try to do otherwise was to risk failure, criticism, and perhaps dismissal, and Bülow had no desire to lose a position that appealed to his towering self-esteem. He did not, therefore, take unnecessary risks, and this was especially true of the way in which he treated his Emperor. In his diary, General von Waldersee tells of having warned Albert Ballin that Bülow, by supporting all of the Emperor's enthusiasms, no matter how dangerous or destructive of good relations with other powers, and by never criticizing or opposing his wishes, was encouraging William II to overestimate his own abilities.

* What one recognized clearly in him was the lack of intelligence. Otherwise, he possessed all the virtues needed for the conduct of business.

[47] G.P., xviii, 2, 840; Graf Pückler in *Front wider Bülow,* pp. 50 ff., Fischer, *ibid.,* p. 390.

Ballin refused to believe this, arguing that the Emperor was too clever to be taken in by crude flattery. Later, Waldersee records, Ballin returned and admitted that he had been wrong. "Bülow," he said, "is a misfortune for us and is destroying the Emperor completely."[48]

What was failing in Bülow, it is clear from all of this, was a sense of responsibility and the basic principles and beliefs from which such a sense might arise. In his perceptive essay on "Bülow as a Man of Letters," R. C. Muschler points out that, to judge from his writings, Bülow had neither religious faith nor genuine patriotism nor any other philosophy except egoism. His letters "drip with citations from the Bible" and are "stuffed with pleas or thanks to God," but there is no sense of any real faith, and one gathers that Bülow used the name of God partly as an ornament and partly as a means of adding weight to his never very substantial reflections. On the other hand, he rarely spoke of his country at all. In hundreds of letters, Muschler tells us, there is no reference to Germany or the fatherland. "It is always a matter only of individuals. . . . Germany? That was just a thing with which he worked."[49] Nothing, in short, impressed Bülow sufficiently to evoke in him a sense of duty toward it; and, this being the case, the only responsibility that he recognized was to himself; and his standards weren't very high.

There is no better illustration of Bülow's spiritual poverty or, for that matter, his essential superficiality and lack of courage, than that notorious comedy of errors called the Daily Telegraph Affair. This arose from the publication, in an English newspaper, of certain statements made by the Emperor about England, her conduct of the Boer war, her allies, and Anglo-German relations, some of which were silly and all of which were impolitic and calculated to inflame the English hostility. On this occasion, however, the Emperor had not acted irresponsibly or in an unconstitutional manner. Before authorizing publication, he had, as recent exhaustive studies of this affair show,[50] sent a copy of the statement to Bülow for

---

[48] Generalfeldmarschall Alfred Graf von Waldersee, *Denkwürdigkeiten,* edited by H. O. Meisner (3 vols., Stuttgart, 1923-25), III, 176, 220.

[49] *Front wider Bülow,* pp. 369 ff.

[50] Wilhelm Schüssler, *Die Daily-Telegraph-Affaire: Fürst Bülow, Kaiser Wilhelm und die Krise des zweiten Reiches 1908* (Göttingen, 1952); Hiller von Gaertringen, *Bülows Denkwürdigkeiten,* Teil II.

his approval. Without reading it, the Chancellor handed it on to subordinates in the Foreign Ministry, with orders that they should look it over "for necessary corrections, additions or omissions."[51] With a lack of imagination and perhaps a disinclination to look for trouble that tells much about the decline of standards in the Wilhelmine civil service, those officials merely checked for factual accuracy and made no judgment as to the political advisability of publication.[52] Nor did Bülow, when the document came back to him. He returned it to the Emperor, and it was mailed to England and published.

When the inevitable uproar began, Bülow was confronted with the alternatives of taking upon himself the responsibility for the publication—and thus revealing what the Austrian ambassador called the *cascade de négligeances*[53] that had gone before—or claiming that he knew nothing of the matter. He seems to have made his choice solely on the basis of how his personal reputation and position would be affected; and, in the Reichstag debate, he managed to obscure the events that preceded publication of the interview while intimating that he disapproved of the interview as such, adding that he was sure that the Emperor had meant well and would be more reticent in the future. If this were not so, he said blandly, neither he nor any of his successors could accept the responsibility of office. It was a masterful performance, in Bülow's best manner, and it was received well; but the fluttering hands and delicate modulations of voice no longer had the power to hide the ugly fact that he nowhere admitted his heavy share in the blame for what had happened and the uglier suspicion that this omission resulted from lack of courage.[54]

In retrospect, the Daily Telegraph Affair seems picayune, although it did more to harm Anglo-German relations than anything since the Krüger dispatch. As a contribution to the coming of the First World War, it is probably less important than another of Bülow's actions, which cannot be discussed here—his approval, in

[51] *Ibid.*, p. 130.
[52] *Ibid.*, pp. 140-144.
[53] Schüssler, *Daily-Telegraph-Affaire*, p. 27.
[54] See Theodor Eschenburg, *Das Kaiserreich am Scheideweg: Bassermann, Bülow und der Block* (Berlin, 1925), pp. 149 f.; Hiller von Gaertringen, *Bülows Denkwürdigkeiten*, pp. 165-172.

January 1909, of a letter from the Chief of the German General
Staff to his opposite number in Austria, giving assurances of support
which changed the whole nature of Germany's commitment under
the Dual Alliance of 1879.[55] But the Daily Telegraph Affair does
throw into sharp relief the distinguishing features of Bülow's statecraft: its superficiality, its lack of energy and courage, its reliance
on theatrical gestures to avoid harsh realities, and—basic to all of
those—its essential irresponsibility.

III

About the third of these Wilhelmine statesmen, Alfred von Kiderlen-Wächter, less need be said; although the high praise lavished
on him by his contemporaries entitles him to some consideration.
Kiderlen-Wächter was the last German diplomat of first rank to
have had an intimate relationship with Bismarck. He had entered the
foreign service in 1879 and served his apprenticeship under a number of able chiefs of mission, including two of Bismarck's "Great
Ambassadors," Münster in Paris (with whom Kiderlen did not get
on) and Radowitz in Constantinople (with whom he did). Holstein
had marked him down as a coming man in the mid-1880's,[56]
and Bismarck himself called him to the Foreign Ministry as an
Eastern expert in 1888 and was soon describing him as "a
useful young man with a practical view."[57] The old Chancellor was,
indeed, so favorably impressed by Kiderlen's talents that he assigned him as a Foreign Ministry counsellor to Emperor William II
during the Emperor's annual northern cruise; and Kiderlen held this
coveted position for ten years, meanwhile moving up the professional ladder and, through his friendship with Holstein, exercising
a not inconsiderable influence in the Foreign Ministry. In 1898, he
fell a victim to the vicious infighting between rival groups in the
Emperor's entourage and had to undergo what was virtual exile in
the legation of Bucharest until 1910. He was never entirely forgotten, however. In 1907 and 1908, he was sent on special missions to

[55] See Craig, *Politics of the Prussian Army*, pp. 286-290.
[56] Rogge, *Holstein und Hohenlohe*, pp. 223, 225, 229, 232.
[57] Jäckh, *Kiderlen-Wächter*, i, 86.

Constantinople; at the height of the Bosnian crisis, he was called to Berlin to be Acting State Secretary for Foreign Affairs; and finally, in 1910, that appointment was made permanent.[58]

Kiderlen, as this sketch of his career shows, could rightly claim to be a Bismarckian by origin and training; it was perhaps only natural that his supporters should claim he was Bismarckian in a deeper sense, that he was indeed a *Bismarck redivivus*. Such a claim was made by Friedrich Naumann, although he cautiously added the adjective "Swabian" before the honored name. Others were less circumspect; and, on Kiderlen's sixtieth birthday, the *Hamburger Nachrichten* draped the great Chancellor's mantle around his shoulders by writing that, measured "by the standards of received Bismarckian tradition," he was the first foreign minister Germany had found since 1890.[59]

One suspects that this sort of thing was a reflection of the poverty of diplomatic talent in Wilhelmine Germany, for surely these statements—and others that claimed that Kiderlen would have prevented the coming of war if it had not been for his untimely death in 1912[60]—are justified by nothing that Kiderlen ever did, or even wrote. Bülow's memoirs are, doubtless, deplorable, but they are at least written with zest. The published papers of Kiderlen show the drafting skill of the Bismarck school and analytical gifts of a high order but, aside from that, they are thin to the point of emaciation. It is hard to disagree with Andreas' judgment that one must conclude the papers that

> what [Kiderlen] wished and what he did stemmed neither from an overwhelmingly humane creativity, nor from intellectual depth, nor from a glowing dedication to a high task. In outstanding statesmen, however coolly and modestly they proceed with the choice of their methods and weapons, there is a holy fire, and Hegel was right in saying that nothing great in the world is done without passion.

[58] *Ibid.*, I, 96 ff. and *passim*; II, 79 ff. See also Haller, *Eulenburg*, I, 182 ff. In December 1908, when Kiderlen became Acting State Secretary, Bülow wrote to Holstein: "I consider K. to have the best political head in our service, and in addition he is a tireless worker." *Holstein Papers*, IV, no. 1163.

[59] Jäckh, *Kiderlen-Wächter*, I, 156 f.

[60] Richard von Kühlmann, quoted in G. P. Gooch, *Studies in Diplomacy* (London, 1942), p. 83.

This Kiderlen lacked and, because he did so, he was a mere *Routinier*.[61].

But let us push this a step further. What does the student of the origins of the First World War remember of Kiderlen-Wächter? Two things: that at the height of the Bosnian crisis of 1908-1909 he dispatched an ultimatum to the Russian government, insisting that it give unequivocal recognition of Austria's acquisition of Bosnia or face the consequences; and that, in 1911, in an attempt to force the French government to give territorial compensation to Germany for tolerating French gains in Morocco, he sent the gunboat *Panther* to Agadir. In both cases, threats were employed as instruments of diplomatic pressure and, it must be added, employed injudiciously, since in the first case the threat was unnecessary (the Russians having already decided to accept the unavoidable), while in the second the menaces could not be expected to accomplish the purpose for which they were used. And these two incidents, which succeeded only in strengthening the ties that bound together Germany's potential antagonists, suggest that Kiderlen's weakness lay not only in the lack of the kind of passion that Bismarck devoted to his calling but in the fact that what passion he possessed he expended in what has been called "sterile excitation,"[62] in fruitless and self-defeating displays of violence.

This conclusion is supported by other evidence. Lancken, who was holding talks with French officials in Paris during the Agadir crisis, has written that Kiderlen was so determined to be firm that he showed a complete disregard for the possibilities of amicable settlement.[63] Hammann tells us that Chancellor Bethmann-Hollweg was always terrified by Kiderlen's willfulness.[64] And even Kiderlen's admiring biographer has supplied corroborative material, in his repeated references to Kiderlen's *Führernatur* and his belief that problems could be solved only by the *Führerpersönlichkeit* (terms, incidentally, that sound more ominous to a post-Hitler generation than they probably did to readers in the 1920's, when the memoirs were published)

[61] W. Andreas, "Kiderlen-Wächter: Randglossen zu seinem Nachlass," *Historische Zeitschrift,* cxxxii (1925), 250 f.
[62] *From Max Weber,* p. 115.
[63] Lancken, *Dienstjahre,* pp. 99 ff.
[64] Hammann, *Bilder,* pp. 86 ff.

and in his further admission that Kiderlen believed that the important thing in life was whether one was *"ein Kerl*—a tough guy."[65] One is forced to conclude that, despite his good qualities—which showed to advantage in his service at Constantinople and Bucharest, and also in the negotiations during the first Balkan war —Kiderlen was too often the kind of diplomat Hindenburg was thinking about when he told Stresemann in 1923 that what Germany needed was more diplomats who knew how to pound their fists upon the table.[66] Germany has had a lot of diplomats like that since 1890, but they have not served her well.

IV

A generation of Epigoni, Monts called Wilhelmine Germany; and, when one considers the statecraft of Holstein, Bülow, and Kiderlen, the classical reference assumes meaning. The disaster that was to overwhelm the nation was not, of course, solely the fault of the diplomats; to say so would be to deny the constitutional and social realities of Imperial Germany. But that the diplomats contributed to the fateful deterioration of Germany's position after 1890 there can be no doubt; and they did so because they no longer held the values and possessed the qualities that inspired the statecraft of their great predecessor.

[65] Jäckh, *Kiderlen-Wächter*, II, 82 ff., 90 ff., 93. Baroness Spitzemberg spoke of Kiderlen's "rudeness," which she said alienated his own colleagues, and of his *"schnöddriges* manner of speech" in negotiation. *Das Tagebuch von Baronin Spitzemberg*, pp. 538, 546.

[66] K. D. Erdmann, "Das Problem der Ost- oder Westorientierung in der Locarno Politik Stresemanns," *Geschichte in Wissenschaft und Unterricht*, VI (1955), 152.

chapter three

THREE REPUBLICAN STATESMEN:

Rathenau, Stresemann, Bruening

DIPLOMACY IS SOMETIMES defined as the art of the possible; and to think of it in this light and to recognize the different factors that restrict a statesman's freedom to choose among possible courses of action helps to illuminate some of the difficulties and the limitations of statecraft. But it should never be forgotten that there are historical situations—usually in time of national defeat and disaster—in which statesmen are not given the privilege of choice at all, but are forced to accept things that they do not wish to accept, or to do things that they do not wish to do, because the penalty for refusing to do so is unacceptable.

What is the role of diplomacy at such moments? Surely it is to make a virtue of necessity. Surely the statesman, at these times, must try to accept the inescapable and undertake the unavoidable in such a way as to derive the greatest possible credit for doing so, both from his antagonists and from other interested parties. Surely he must exploit all the circumstances of his act of capitulation in order to win positive benefit from it. In such circumstances, in other words, diplomacy becomes a matter of making the best of a bad situation. It becomes the art of the necessary.[1]

[1] W. W. Schütz has written an article entitled "Politik als Kunst des Notwendigen," in *Aussenpolitik,* VII (1956), 495 ff., but he gives the concept a different meaning than I have here.

In the years that followed Germany's collapse in 1918, the new republican government was faced with the hard necessity of accepting the burden of the Paris peace terms. To have refused to do so was hardly within the realm of practical politics, for the Allies made it clear that they were prepared to renew the war, if necessary, in order to enforce their will. Responsible German statesmen had, therefore, to accept the necessary, hoping that the way in which they went about doing this—that is, the very process of negotiation involved in bowing to the inevitable and implementing it—might lighten their prospective burdens and modify their incurred obligations.

It was not, of course, easy to take even the first step in this dubious enterprise. Germany's defeat had created a new political situation in which the government and its agencies were subject to a much greater degree of control by public opinion, on the one hand, and by parliament and the parties, on the other, than had been true before the war. It had also left significant sections of the German population in a resentful and rebellious mood, unreconciled to the disaster that had befallen their country, indisposed to make any concessions to the victors, and incapable of appreciating the realities with which their ministers had to grapple. To do what reason of state required without alienating public opinion was virtually impossible, as the careers of Rathenau, Stresemann, and Bruening demonstrate.

I

With Richard II, Walter Rathenau might well have said

> I am sworn brother . . .
> To grim Necessity; and he and I
> Will keep a league till death.

He was the first postwar statesman to face squarely up to the realities of Germany's position and to base his policy and his diplomacy upon acceptance of the necessary. And for this he paid with his life at the hands of assassins in November 1922.

The very fact that Walter Rathenau could serve as Foreign Minister of Germany illustrates the social transformation wrought by the establishment of the republic and the change in the nature of foreign affairs caused by the enhanced importance of economic ques-

tions. For Rathenau was not only a Jew but one who proudly refused
to be converted, a fact that would automatically have excluded him
from the higher branches of the state service under the imperial
regime. At the same time, as the son of Emil Rathenau, the founder
of the Allgemeine-Elektrizitäts-Gesellschaft (A.E.G.), and as part
owner or director of eighty-six German and twenty-one foreign enter-
prises in his own right, Rathenau symbolized the role that large-scale
business was now to play in international politics.[2]

To deal with the complicated economic aspects of German postwar
policy, Rathenau was well qualified. He had demonstrated his abilities in the superb manner in which he had organized and administered the War Raw Materials Department during the first half of
the war,[3] as well as in a series of writings in which he foresaw the
economic disintegration that would inevitably follow that conflict
and the degree to which general recovery would depend upon an
integrated approach to the problems that would face Germany and
her neighbors.[4] To be sure, he saw those problems, and their solutions, at first through the rose-colored glasses of inevitable German
victory and domination, for not until November 1918 did he imagine
the defeat of his country possible, and even then he rejected the
idea.[5] But, even in his disillusionment, he never wavered in his belief that the big problems of the future would be economic ones
and that they must be handled on a European scale. His fore-
sight in this respect was clearer than that of some Allied statesmen.

Vision—upon which Rathenau himself put a high valuation,
claiming that "the ability to imagine what has not yet happened"
was the mark of the outstanding statesman[6]—is an important gift,
but it is not everything. In Rathenau's case, it and his undeniable

[2] Count Harry Kessler, *Walther Rathenau: His Life and Work* (New
York, 1930), pp. 48 ff., 117, 122.

[3] See, *inter alia*, Eric Kollmann, "Walther Rathenau and German Foreign
Policy: Thoughts and Actions," *Journal of Modern History*, xxiv (1952),
129 f.; Kessler, *Rathenau*, pp. 171 ff.

[4] Kollmann in *Journal of Modern History*, xxiv, 128-130; Henry Cord
Meyer, *Mitteleuropa in German Thought and Action* (The Hague, 1955),
pp. 139-140. Colonel House spoke of Rathenau's "clear vision" and "prophetic
forecast as to the future." *Intimate Papers of Colonel House* (4 vols., Boston,
1926 ff.), I, 402.

[5] Kollmann in *Journal of Modern History*, xxiv, 132.

[6] Margarete von Eynern in her introduction to *Walther Rathenau: Ein
preussischer Europäer: Briefe* (Berlin, 1955), p. 22.

technical abilities were both offset to some extent by personal short-comings. The very fertility of his imagination made it easier for him to formulate new schemes than to hold firm to established ones, and the art of digging one's heels in was not highly developed in him.[7] He was also a moody man, given to fits of profound discourage-ment, a dangerous tendency in a statesman, because it lends itself to exploitation by others.[8] These traits were to reveal themselves in his diplomacy, sometimes at inconvenient moments.

Simultaneously, Rathenau had a penchant for a kind of aestheti-cism and mysticism that was not readily understood by ordinary minds and was easily misinterpreted by malicious ones.[9] Finally, despite his refusal to abandon the faith of his fathers, he was ashamed of being a Jew and idealized the very blond, blue-eyed Teutons who were most apt to find his writings incomprehensible, his inordi-nate personal vanity ridiculous, and—once he had become Foreign Minister—his Jewishness an insult to the nation.[10] These charac-teristics made it unlikely that he would ever command popular support, although—to do him justice—it must be remembered that the nature of the policy he had to follow would probably have made that impossible in any case.

Whatever his other failings, it cannot be denied that Rathenau had political courage; and this he demonstrated from the moment he re-entered politics in 1920, as a member of the German delegation to the Spa conference. At this gathering, which was called to discuss German disarmament[11] and reparations, and which was held in an atmosphere of indescribable bitterness and tenseness,[12] the German representatives were presented with a demand for deliveries of coal to an amount of 2,000,000 tons monthly for a period of six months

---

[7] Wipert von Blücher, *Deutschlands Weg nach Rapallo* (Wiesbaden, 1951), pp. 156 f.

[8] See Gerald Freund, *Unholy Alliance* (New York, 1957), p. 105.

[9] Erich Eyck, *Geschichte der Weimarer Republik* (2 vols., Zurich, 1954-56), I, 250. Herbert von Dirksen spoke of the "breath of decadence" that emanated from Rathenau. *Moskau, Tokio, London: Erinnerungen und Betrachtungen zu 20 Jahren deutscher Aussenpolitik, 1919-1939* (Stuttgart, 1950), p. 44.

[10] On this, see especially M. J. Bonn, *Wandering Scholar* (New York, 1948), pp. 265 f.

[11] The military aspect of the Spa conference is discussed in Craig, *Politics of the Prussian Army*, pp. 389-392.

[12] See Carl Bergmann, *The History of Reparations* (London, 1927), pp. 40 f.

from 1 August 1920; and it was made clear that, in case of default, the Allies would occupy the Ruhr. Confronted with an ultimatum of this kind it was perhaps easier to strike attitudes of outraged and defiant patriotism, as the coal magnate Hugo Stinnes did at Spa, than to adopt the unpopular but necessary course. Stinnes, whom Josef Wirth once called a *Katastrophenpolitiker*, wanted to defy the Allies even at the cost of new sanctions, for he confidently expected that the subsequent advance of Bolshevism, which new hardship would invite, would soon bring the British and French to terms.[13] Rathenau opposed this as chimerical and irresponsible and persuaded the delegation to accept the ultimatum.

He did not do so in a spirit of submissiveness or resignation, or even for the mere sake of saving the Ruhr. Had he had his way, the government, while yielding, would have sought to define the total reparations liability by offering to pay a definite amount. This might not have been accepted, but it would probably have led to further negotiations, and Rathenau, like Talleyrand, believed that, once negotiations are possible, anything is possible. Lord d'Abernon was to write later: "[Rathenau] has taken to international conferences with passion. He wants them to go on all the time."[14] This was true. In Germany's present plight, negotiations alone, Rathenau thought, offered an ascent from the depths into which defeat had plunged her. For in negotiations one must deal with concrete issues rather than with prejudices and passions, and, in doing so, one may discover unexpected areas of agreement. Rathenau put his faith in the process, hoping that modest agreements might lead to more ambitious ones until at last the "iron curtain" (as it was called in the 1920's),[15] which existed between Germany and the West, fell completely before the onslaught of practical men.[16]

[13] Stinnes' conduct at Spa is described in Edgar Viscount d'Abernon, *An Ambassador of Peace* (3 vols., London, 1929-30), I, 64 ff.; and Harold Nicolson, *Curzon: The Last Phase, 1919-1925* (new edition, New York, 1939), pp. 226-230. See also Harry Graf Kessler, *Tagebücher* (Frankfurt am Main, 1962), p. 559, and Günter Schubert, *Anfänge nationalsozialistischer Aussenpolitik* (Köln, 1963), p. 182.

[14] D'Abernon, *Ambassador of Peace*, I, 255.

[15] For uses of the term in the 1920's, see *ibid.*, III, 101, 211; and Gustav Stresemann, *Vermächtnis*, edited by H. Bernhard (3 vols., Berlin, 1932-33), III, 327. It was often used with specific reference to the demilitarized zone.

[16] On Rathenau's faith in negotiation, see Kessler, *Rathenau*, pp. 276-277.

This remained Rathenau's faith after he had become Minister of Reconstruction in the cabinet of Josef Wirth in 1921, at a time when the Allies themselves had defined the total extent of German reparations and demanded German agreement. In his first speech to the Reichstag, Rathenau once more argued for acceptance and scrupulous fulfillment of the Allied terms, reminding his auditors of the Beethoven quartet movement [Op. 135, the final movement] that "begins with slow tones 'Must it be?' and closes with a decided and powerful 'It must be!' " "Whoever comes to his task without that 'It must be'!" Rathenau added, "comes to his task without the solution" of Germany's problems.[17]

Here again, Rathenau's view was not simply negative. The significant passage in this speech was that in which he said, "We must find ways to bring ourselves together again with the world!"[18] It was his hope that, sooner or later, Germany's act of yielding to necessity, and her honest fulfillment of the terms imposed, would be repaid by a willingness on the part of the Allies at least to talk about new forms of reparations payment; and, as Minister of Reconstruction and, after February 1922, as Foreign Minister, all his efforts were bent towards finding opportunities for fruitful interchange. Nor were they completely unsuccessful. The Wiesbaden agreement of October 1921, which he negotiated with Louis Loucheur, had perhaps almost insignificant economic results, but its political importance—its demonstration of the possibility of bilateral Franco-German negotiations—was certainly not negligible.[19] The concessions won from the Allies at the abortive Cannes conference were, however minor, still a testimony to growing Allied sympathy for German difficulties and confidence in her good intentions.[20] These were indications, however slight, that Rathenau was, in fact, succeeding in his policy of making a virtue of necessity.

In view of this, it is unfortunate that his brief term as Foreign Minister should have culminated, not in another modest step towards reconciliation with the West, but in a sensational event that

---

[17] Walther Rathenau, *Gesammelte Reden* (Berlin, 1924), p. 203.

[18] *Ibid.*, p. 200.

[19] See Bergmann, *Reparations*, pp. 92-96; Eyck, *Geschichte*, I, 253; Kollmann in *Journal of Modern History*, XXIV, 135; Kessler, *Rathenau*, pp. 291 ff.; and Schubert, *Anfänge*, pp. 189 f.

[20] Kessler, *Rathenau*, pp. 297 ff.; Bergmann, *Reparations*, pp. 113 ff.

ran counter to his previous policy. The story of the Genoa conference of 1922 has often been told; and the high hopes with which the Germans went to Genoa, their failure to establish contact with the British, their growing fear that an Allied-Soviet pact might be concluded at their expense, the adroitness with which the Soviets exploited this fear, and the eventual signing of the Soviet-German treaty of friendship at Rapallo form a familiar story.[21] What is not known, and probably cannot be known with any assurance, is what the Germans might have gained at Genoa if it had *not* been for Rapallo. Marcus Wallenberg, the Swedish financier, later claimed that the news of Rapallo had frustrated a plan for the rehabilitation of German finances that had been worked out by English, Dutch, and Swedish experts, had the approval of the British Treasury, and provided for a large international loan to Germany as the first step toward a definitive reparations settlement.[22] Even if one refuses to believe that anything so ambitious could have come through the shoals of negotiation at Genoa, the Germans would probably have made some gains, especially since their fears of a separate Soviet-Western deal at their expense were completely groundless. Instead, the Rapallo treaty put a stop to whatever progress had been made towards Allied-German understanding, irritated the British and infuriated the French, and contributed to the mood that led to the invasion of the Ruhr in January 1923.[23]

Baron Maltzan, the head of the Eastern Division of the German Foreign Ministry and an enthusiast for Soviet-German ties, talking later in private about the way in which he had persuaded Rathenau to sign the Rapallo treaty, boasted that he had "raped" the Foreign

[21] See, *inter alia*, J. Saxon Mills, *The Genoa Conference* (New York, 1922); Viscount Swinton, *I Remember* (London, 1946), pp. 17-25; A. J. Sylvester, *The Real Lloyd George* (London, 1947), pp. 80-98; Amedeo Giannini, *Saggi di storia diplomatica, 1920-40* (Firenze, 1940), pp. 27-50; Jane Degras, *Soviet Documents on Foreign Policy*, 1 (Oxford, 1951), 287-318; Louis Fischer, *The Soviets in World Affairs* (new edition, 2 vols., Princeton, 1951), 1, 318-354; Kessler, *Rathenau*, pp. 304-340; Freund, *Unholy Alliance*, pp. 111 ff.; W. Freiherr von Rheinbaben, "Deutsche Ostpolitik in Locarno," *Aussenpolitik*, IV (1953), 35 f.; Theodor Schieder, "Die Probleme des Rapallo-Vertrags," *Arbeitsgemeinschaft für Forschung des Landes Nordrhein-Westfalen: Geisteswissenschaften*, Heft 43 (Köln, 1956), pp. 33 ff.; Herbert Helbig, *Die Träger der Rapallo Politik* (Göttingen, 1958).

[23] For the views of President Ebert and R. Nadolny, *ibid.*, pp. 159, 163.

[22] W. von Blücher, *Rapallo*, p. 164 n.

Minister.[24] One suspects that Rathenau's personality supplies a better explanation for his submissiveness. Lord d'Abernon always believed that Rapallo had its origins in the fact that Rathenau's vanity had been outraged by Lloyd George's disregard; and this may well be true.[25] It is even more likely, however, that, after his cool reception by the Allies, Rathenau's powerful imagination summoned up illusory but terrifying dangers, while his tendency to discouragement asserted itself, and made him surrender fatalistically to what his experts told him was a means of saving something from the shipwreck of his hopes.[26] Much has been written about Rapallo restoring independence to German foreign policy, but it is hard to prove that this or any other tangible benefit came from Rathenau's action, which was, all things considered, an act of weakness and a denial of everything he had accomplished so far.[27]

Perhaps this is unfair. Rathenau's great service to his country was to have seen and accepted the necessity of the fulfillment policy and to have followed it persistently, despite the frantic mouthings of patrioteers, who blamed him for the depreciation of the currency and the pulverization of the middle class, and the billingsgate of the Fuehrer of the National Socialist party who, in March 1922, had publicly denounced "Rathenau, the *Judensau*" for having "betrayed and sold the German people."[28] Even after Rapallo he pursued his

[24] *Ibid.,* p. 161 n.; Freund, *Unholy Alliance,* p. 119. Cf. Dirksen, *Moskau, Tokio, London,* p. 46.

[25] D'Abernon, *Ambassador of Peace,* i, 308 ff. Bonn suggests that Lloyd George's disregard was prompted by the fact that "the repetitive melancholy of this male Cassandra [Rathenau] depressed his springy optimism. . . . Mr. Lloyd George had frankly got bored." *Wandering Scholar,* p. 267.

[26] *Ibid.,* p. 269. Rathenau had apparently believed for some time that nothing really permanent could be accomplished in the reparations question until something drastic—a Poincaré ministry and an invasion of the Ruhr, for instance—had occurred. He seems, in short, to have been in a pessimistic mood, even before Genoa. See Kollmann in *Journal of Modern History,* xxiv (1952), 136. After Genoa, he told Otto Gessler that an occupation of the Ruhr was unavoidable. Otto Gessler, *Reichswehrpolitik in der Weimarer Zeit,* edited by Kurt Sendtner (Stuttgart, 1958), p. 239.

[27] See Hans von Raumer, "Dreissig Jahre nach Rapallo," *Deutsche Rundschau,* 78. Jahrgang (1952), 321 ff.; Felix Stössinger, "Die Wahrheit über Rapallo," *ibid.,* 550 ff.; R. K., "Der Mythus von Rapallo: In Wirklichkeit war das meist ganz anders," *Deutsche Zeitung und Wirtschaftszeitung,* 26 June 1954, p. 3.

[28] Eyck, *Geschichte,* i, 285 f.; and Schubert, *Anfänge,* p. 191.

way, until assassination put an end to his efforts. If his achievement was small, and if this was partly because of the deficiencies of his diplomacy, it was at least a beginning to the work that Gustav Stresemann was to carry further.[29]

II

The second and much greater of these three republican statesmen suffered from none of the character traits that had blemished his predecessor's achievement. There was nothing exotic in Stresemann's appearance or mannerisms, no trace of aestheticism in his tastes, no mystical strain in his thought. His literary preferences and his views on general subjects did not differ greatly from those of the petty bourgeoisie from which he had come;[30] and, while he was capable of rising to heights of poetic eloquence in his essays and speeches, this facilitated his ability to reach the minds of his audience instead of reducing it, as Rathenau's more involved rhetoric had done. (Not everyone was favorably affected by these gifts, of course. Theodor Heuss admitted in his memoirs that he could never stand Stresemann's sentimentality, and it was perhaps for that reason that he excluded the Republic's most distinguished statesman from the series *Great Germans,* which he edited, with Hermann Heimpel and Benno Reiffenberg, after the war.) From the fits of gloom into which his predecessor had fallen, Stresemann was protected by a natural optimism and great resilience. Moreover, if in his private life he was inclined to be oversensitive to fancied slights and resentful at supposed affronts, he rigorously suppressed considerations of personal vanity in his conduct of foreign affairs and showed himself capable of supporting the most mortifying blows (the League's refusal to admit Germany to membership in the Council in the spring of 1926,

[29] On the similarity of Stresemann's policies to those of Rathenau, see Kollmann in *Journal of Modern History,* xxiv (1952), 141. For another appreciation of the totality of Rathenau's work, see Hans von Raumer, "Walther Rathenau," *Deutsche Rundschau,* 78. Jahrgang (1952), 664 ff.

[30] Annelise Thimme, *Gustav Stresemann: Eine politische Biographie zur Geschichte der Weimarer Republik* (Hannover and Frankfurt-am-Main, 1957), p. 14. He even shared that class's admiration for Bülow, whom he once called "the greatest living German statesman." *Ibid.,* p. 29.

for instance) with calm, if not equanimity. *"So ist das Leben,"* he said on one occasion. "We must take men and peoples and things as they are."[31]

The kind of courage that is needed to admit the inevitable and accept it, Stresemann, like Rathenau, possessed to a high degree. He gave evidence of this as early as the war years, when he finally came around to supporting a basic reform of the Prussian franchise, a position which, it might be added, it was not easy for him to adopt, in view of his convictions and his connections. But, as he wrote to one of the leaders of his party on that occasion: "There are moments in which one must have the courage to seize the rudder and give the ship a definite course, even if a new one; and I am firmly convinced that this last decision of ours was a necessity. . . ."[32]

Six years later, when Stresemann was having his short one hundred days as Chancellor of the Reich, courage of that order was needed in even greater degree. For in that tragic autumn of 1923 the process begun with the French invasion of the Ruhr came to full crisis, and the country was gripped in the throes of economic disorganization and domestic revolution. At this juncture, Stresemann made what was probably the bravest and certainly the most painful decision of his life, the decision to capitulate to the French by terminating the policy of passive resistance that was contributing so heavily to the disintegration of the social fabric.

When Stresemann took that difficult step, he was assailed by the patriotic press; and one newspaper wrote that he deserved to be brought to trial for treason. The Chancellor's answer deserves to be quoted.

> I am prepared and happy [he said] to take my stand before any tribunal to defend what I have done. . . . Giving up passive resistance is perhaps more patriotic than the phrases with which it is combated. I knew when I did it . . . that I was putting my own political position in my party—yes, and even my life—in jeopardy. But what

[31] Annelise Thimme, "Gustav Stresemann, Legende und Wirklichkeit," *Historische Zeitschrift,* CLXXXI (1956), 313 f. Stresemann's optimism led Monts to call him a "second Bülow" and aroused Hindenburg's distrust. Gessler, *Reichswehrpolitik,* pp. 314, 349.

[32] Thimme in *Historische Zeitschrift,* CLXXXI (1956), 295. On Stresemann's activity during the war, see Marvin L. Edwards, *Stresemann and the Greater Germany* (New York, 1962).

is it that we Germans lack? We lack the courage to take responsibility.[33]

The point has already been made that willingness to retreat from an impossible position, however courageous it may be, does not in itself constitute statecraft. It was Stresemann's ability to exploit the act of surrender, and to make the most of the circumstances created by it, that made him an outstanding practitioner of the kind of diplomacy that has been called here the art of the necessary. This deserves closer attention.

The abandonment of passive resistance helped to win the sympathy of important groups in Great Britain and other countries; and this, together with the growing concern felt over the distress caused throughout western Europe by the disruption of the German economy, led to the talks in which the Dawes Plan was formulated. By German patriots this plan was attacked as a demand for a new surrender, a reaction that Stresemann viewed with contempt. The goal of all of Germany's efforts, he felt, should be the regaining of her political and economic freedom; and the Dawes Plan was an essential step in that direction. It would bring to Germany the international credits without which the fulfillment of her reparations obligation would be impossible; and, unless reparations payments were resumed, the Ruhr would not be evacuated. These considerations alone justified acceptance of the plan. In addition, it seemed obvious to Stresemann that, with the passage of time, the plan would make Germany's creditors increasingly dependent upon her, since, once they were committed to giving her financial assistance, they could not remain unaffected if she were again threatened by disaster. In that growing dependence, Stresemann saw great opportunity for his country. As he said in a speech in December 1925: "One must simply have . . . so many debts that the creditor sees his own existence jeopardized if the debtor collapses. . . . These economic matters create bridges of political understanding and future political support."[34]

[33] Quoted in Martin Göhring, *Stresemann, Mensch, Staatsmann, Europäer: Gedenkrede, gehalten am 8. Juli 1956* (Mainz, 1956), pp. 19 f. On Stresemann's course during this crisis, see particularly Henry L. Turner, *Stresemann and the Politics of the Weimar Republic* (Princeton, 1963), pp. 114 ff.

[34] Thimme, *Stresemann*, p. 69 and *Historische Zeitschrift*, CLXXXI, 314. For the kind of arguments Stresemann advanced in public, see *Vermächtnis*, I, 418 ff. It is interesting to note that, at a meeting of the ministers of state

These calculations, which dictated Stresemann's successful fight
for the plan, were in the long run correct. In addition, the financial
talks of 1924 created an atmosphere in which the Allies became
accustomed to talking with the Germans as equals again and in
which they were not unwilling to give consideration to German proposals of new subjects of negotiation. It was precisely because of
this new climate that Stresemann was able to accomplish his diplomatic masterpiece, the negotiation at Locarno of the Rhineland
Pact, which by securing Germany's western frontier made a repetition of the Ruhr invasion impossible, and the agreement by which
Germany was admitted into the League of Nations under conditions
that freed her from any obligation to participate in a war between
the Soviet Union and the other powers.

As a diplomat Stresemann possessed three great gifts, which were
seen at their best in the Locarno period. These were his ability to
sense danger and to avoid it by seizing and retaining the initiative;
his ability to maintain his perspective and his sense of values in the
midst of a changing diplomatic situation; and, finally, his ability to
be more stubborn than his partners in negotiation and to refuse to
allow their importunities to force him to accept second-best solutions.

With respect to the first of these, it might be remarked that it
was Stresemann who took the initiative in proposing negotiations
for a Rhineland pact and that, in doing so, he was motivated by a
lively apprehension concerning what might happen if he merely
waited upon events. For in the fall of 1924 the MacDonald government in England fell from office, and the Foreign Secretary in the
new Conservative Cabinet was Austen Chamberlain, the tendencies of whose policy Stresemann distrusted[35]—as well he might when
one considers that Chamberlain was reported to have said that he
loved France as one loves a beautiful woman.[36] Shortly thereafter,

---

on 7 April 1933, Foreign Minister von Neurath listed "the interest of our
creditors in our debt" among Germany's assets in foreign affairs. See *Documents on German Foreign Policy, 1918-1945* (Washington, 1949 ff.) [here-
after cited as *German Documents*], series C, I, 257.

[35] The distrust did not fade with the years. At the end of his career,
Stresemann said: "Sir Austen is a gentleman. I know he means well. But for
the last ten years Europe has been suffering from gentlemen who mean well."
R. Bruce Lockhart, *Retreat from Glory* (New York, 1934), pp. 338 ff.

[36] Walter Görlitz, *Gustav Stresemann* (Heidelberg, 1947), p. 208.

the Western powers announced that, because of imperfect German fulfillment of Article 429 of the Versailles Treaty, which specified the conditions of German disarmament, they would not evacuate the first zone of occupation in the Rhineland in January 1925, as had been planned. This seemed to reverse whatever progress had been made, during the financial talks, toward reconciliation between Germany and the West; and Stresemann feared that worse was coming. Chamberlain, he explained later, in a speech before the Foreign Affairs Committee of the Reichstag, was

> at the very least decidedly cool toward us, while on the other hand he had to be counted among the adherents of the *Entente cordiale* with France and of the idea of a guarantee treaty between the Allies that would certainly be directed against us. Moreover, we could reckon that, in view of the British Empire's difficulties in the Near East, a conciliatory disposition toward France in this matter might perhaps be regarded by the English simply as payment for a conciliatory disposition on the part of France in the Near East.[37]

The German Foreign Minister saw the possibility, in short, of a new Anglo-French agreement; he feared that, if it came into existence, it would perpetuate the occupation of the Rhineland and would, at the same time, force the German government to make the unhappy choice between isolation and dependence upon the Soviet Union. To forestall this, therefore, he came forward in January 1925 with his proposal of a pact in which Germany, France, Belgium, Italy, and Great Britain would guarantee the existing Rhineland frontiers;[38] and, despite the initially cool reception that this plan received in London, he repeated the offer in Paris a month later. In diplomacy persistence of this kind often pays dividends, and it did here. In March, the British government—caught between a public demand for some kind of a security pact and their own lack of enthusiasm for the still pending Geneva Protocol (which would require a commitment to oppose aggression wherever it occurred on the Continent)—discovered new virtues in Stresemann's

[37] Quoted in Thimme, *Stresemann*, pp. 80-81. See also Ludwig Zimmermann, *Studien zur Geschichte der Weimarer Republik* (Erlangen, 1956), p. 54; and Erdmann in *Geschichte in Wissenschaft*, VI, 139.
[38] This proposal had, of course, been made before, as early as 1922, by the Cuno government.

regional proposal;[39] and the initiative that the German Foreign Minister had seized at the outset he was now able to retain.

If one studies the subsequent negotiations with an eye to diplomatic method rather than for the purpose of deciding whether or not Stresemann was a "good European" (a much controverted subject that will not be touched on here), one cannot but be impressed by the Foreign Minister's ability to maintain his perspective and his sense of relative values. The price of the pact was the renunciation of Alsace-Lorraine, which seemed treasonable to nationalists at home, but which Stresemann accepted as a foregone conclusion, since the territories renounced were lost in any case. The important thing in his mind was to create a situation in the West that might facilitate the evacuation of the Rhineland without placing limits on Germany's freedom of action in the east. This depended on the defeat of the repeated French attempts to have the guarantee principle extended from Germany's western frontiers to her eastern ones, a defeat that was effected by Stresemann's frank but persistent refusal to enter any engagements in the east and was made definite by the happy accident that the British were equally disinclined to make eastern commitments. After it became clear that Chamberlain was not to be moved from his belief that, for the Polish Corridor, "no British government ever will or ever can risk the bones of a British grenadier,"[40] Stresemann was safe. He could now claim that the Rhineland Pact had drawn the teeth of the Franco-Polish alliance by freeing Germany of the fear of an automatic French attack in the event of a war with Poland in which Germany was not clearly the aggressor;[41] and he could now hope that the successful conclusion of the Locarno treaties would in itself create a psychological atmosphere that would be more favorable to the promotion of Germany's territorial interests in both east and west.[42] And, indeed, the first fruit

[39] See, inter alia, Sir C. Petrie, Life and Letters of the Right Honorable Sir Austen Chamberlain (2 vols., London, 1939-40), II, 258 ff.

[40] R. D. Challener, "The French Foreign Office," in The Diplomats, 1919-1939, edited by Gordon A. Craig and Felix Gilbert (Princeton, 1953), p. 82.

[41] See Thimme in Historische Zeitschrift, CLXXXI, 315 f.; Erdmann in Geschichte in Wissenschaft, VI, 147 ff.; Schieder, "Probleme," p. 57; and Zygmunt J. Gasiorowski, "Stresemann and Poland before Locarno," Journal of Central European Affairs, XVIII (1958), 47.

[42] That Stresemann thought of achieving his eastern ambitions by negotiation and not by force is supported by abundant evidence. He seems to have

of Locarno was the reversal of the earlier decision of the Allies to postpone the evacuation of the first Rhineland zone.

In the parallel negotiations over the conditions under which Germany would enter the League of Nations, Stresemann's principal objective was to secure an exemption from the general liability, imposed by Article 16 of the Covenant, to resort to sanctions in the case of aggression against a League member. Since Germany was not permitted to arm herself as other states did, she could not, he argued, contribute military or economic aid to any joint action against an aggressor or even permit League members taking such action to send their troops across her territory; and, in order to avoid misunderstanding and possible retaliation by nonmembers, this must be made patently clear to all. He was unmoved by the suggestion that objections to Article 16 should properly be discussed only after Germany had entered the League; and he rejected the argument that Germany should be satisfied by the reflection that she could never be forced to participate in sanctions since, as a member of the Council, she would have the right to veto any proposed action. The veto right, he pointed out, was only theoretically a solution to Germany's special problem; in actual practice, the German government would be exposed to moral pressure in every case of contemplated action and to moral isolation if it used the veto.

In taking this position, Stresemann was, of course, thinking of the possibility of a future Soviet attack on Poland. He knew perfectly well that, if the circumstances of Germany's admission to the League made it appear even remotely possible that it might be forced to give aid to the Poles, he would have great difficulty in withstanding nationalist attacks at home and, moreover, would find it impossible to reassure the Russians, who regarded Germany's entrance into the Geneva system as an anti-Soviet gesture and who would not be fobbed off by assurances that Germany's veto right was a guarantee of its future neutrality.

It was, moreover, important to disabuse Western statesmen of any false illusions they might entertain. Stresemann was determined that Germany should not have to pay for admission to the League with

counted on being helped by a total economic collapse of Poland. See Erdmann in *Geschichte in Wissenschaft*, vi, 149-151; Erich Eyck, "Neues Licht auf Stresemanns Politik," *Deutsche Rundschau*, 81. Jahrang (1955), 118; Antonina Vallentin, *Stresemann* (London, 1931), pp. 261 f.

the abandonment of its freedom of action in foreign affairs. He was anxious to secure League membership, because of the obvious opportunities it would provide for promoting his other policy objectives by means of propaganda and negotiation; but membership in the League must not be regarded as superseding other treaty obligations or binding Germany exclusively to the West. "We would not," Stresemann said later to some members of the Nationalist party, "permit ourselves to be used as a tool against Russia; therefore, we insisted on our reservations with respect to the League."[43]

In pressing those reservations, Stresemann—who often said that diplomacy was a matter of compromise—showed himself for once to be completely uncompromising, holding out for an unequivocal exemption before Germany entered the League. Moreover, when his persistence threatened to create an impasse, it was he who offered the way out. Surely, he suggested, Germany's special requirements might be met by an interpretation of Article 16 similar to that made in the Geneva Protocol. That document had included a clause to the effect that the signatory powers were obliged to cooperate against aggressors "to an extent which [was] compatible with their geographical situation and the special state of their armaments." Having failed utterly to move Stresemann from his position, the other negotiators seized thankfully upon this formula; and Germany was permitted to enter the League with the exemption Stresemann had sought—and with no obligation to participate in a future League action against the Soviet Union.[44]

Not the least interesting aspect of this brilliant diplomatic achievement, which, in the words of Lord d'Abernon, raised Germany "from the position of a stricken and disarmed foe into that of a diplomatic equal, entitled to full consideration as a Great Power and enjoying international guarantee for the protection of her frontier,"[45] was Stresemann's behavior toward Moscow before and during the negotiations. In contrast to his predecessor, whose romantic fascination by the Soviet Union was perhaps one more reason for the way in which he was overpowered at Genoa, and in even sharper con-

[43] Hans W. Gatzke, "Von Rapallo nach Berlin: Stresemann und die deutsche Russlandpolitik," *Vierteljahrshefte für Zeitgeschichte*, IV (1956), 9, note 49.
[44] On all this, *ibid.*, pp. 9-19; Erdmann in *Geschichte in Wissenschaft*, VI, 145; Schieder, "Probleme," pp. 63 ff.
[45] D'Abernon, *Ambassador of Peace*, III, 20.

trast to those who, like Brockdorff-Rantzau, had come to believe in a "brotherhood of destiny" between Germany and Soviet Russia, Stresemann's attitude was one of cool reserve; and he was even more determined to preserve his independence vis-à-vis Russia than he was to avoid an exclusive bond with the West. He always remembered that Moscow was the headquarters of the Comintern, and hence the source of many of his political troubles.[46] He admitted the advantage of the secret military collaboration between the two powers, because he appreciated the importance of power in international diplomacy;[47] and he was always in favor of greater economic co-operation with the Russians.[48] But he wanted no closer ties than those that had existed since 1922, for—unlike General von Seeckt, who seems to have desired a military alliance for the sake of destroying Poland —he believed that dependence upon the Soviet Union would result in diplomatic isolation and the communization of Germany.[49] This attitude, and his natural steadiness of nerve in diplomatic intercourse, enabled him to withstand the remarkable campaign of menaces and blandishments that the Russians—supported by such allies as Seeckt and Brockdorff-Rantzau—waged against his Locarno policy. The Soviet desire for another engagement he satisfied with the Berlin Treaty of 1926, but only after the western arrangements had been completed; and the new treaty seems to have represented no more to him than a kind of reaffirmation of his policy of steering a middle course between East and West in order to reassert Germany's influence in Europe.

These comments upon Stresemann's methods would be incomplete if they did not touch in passing on his recognition of the intimate connection between foreign and domestic affairs and the effort he devoted to winning the support of the parties, and public opinion in general, for his policies. In the great crisis of 1923, he had com-

[46] *Vermächtnis*, II, 516.
[47] See especially Hans W. Gatzke, *Stresemann and the Rearmament of Germany* (Baltimore, 1954); and the same author's "Russo-German Military Collaboration during the Weimar Republic," *American Historical Review*, LXIII (1958), 565 ff.
[48] Gatzke in *Vierteljahrshefte*, IV, 28 f.
[49] *Vermächtnis*, II, 553; Thimme, Stresemann, pp. 106 ff.; Erdmann in *Geschichte in Wissenschaft*, VI, 140; Theodor Eschenburg, *Die improvisierte Demokratie: Gesammelte Aufsätze zur Weimarer Republik* (München, 1963), p. 204.

plained that too many people would not understand that "the recovery of a people is not won only by braggadocio and saber-rattling without a saber. . . . The German always sees foreign policy only from the standpoint of domestic party conflicts and thereby loses any sense of what is necessary."[50] But he did not content himself with repining, but threw himself into the task of education and persuasion. For this purpose, as Henry Bretton has pointed out, he drew heavily on American advertising techniques and British propaganda practices; he maintained excellent relations with the press; and he wrote incessantly under his own name and various pseudonyms for magazines and newspapers.[51] Among the parties, and especially within his own badly split party, he followed the line of expediency, being all things to all men and tailoring his tactics and his language to his auditors. This has presented difficulties to those people looking for consistency and sincerity in Stresemann's work;[52] but it was plainly designed to make possible a united and continuous foreign policy and to advance his specific diplomatic objectives.

Despite these methods, it was only with the greatest of difficulty that Stresemann secured continued party and public support. The opening of each phase of his policy was accompanied by new campaigns of defamation and by bitter fights in the Reichstag; and the delays and disappointments that followed Locarno and Thoiry kept his opponents abundantly supplied with ammunition to use against him. It is a tribute to his courage and his unflagging energy that he held to his course until the Hague Conference of 1929 crowned his work by setting a definite date for the evacuation of the Rhineland. A French historian wrote that, at The Hague, Stresemann had put the final touches to the greatest diplomatic masterpiece

---

[50] *Vermächtnis,* I, 221.

[51] Henry L. Bretton, *Stresemann and the Revision of Versailles: A Fight for Reason* (Stanford, 1953), pp. 44-45. Eschenburg calls Stresemann "one of the most gifted publicists among the politicians." *Die improvisierte Demokratie,* p. 146.

[52] See Thimme in *Historische Zeitschrift,* CLXXXI, 302-305, 335 and notes; and her *Stresemann,* pp. 15, 43, 61, 64, 85, 129; and Turner, *Stresemann,* chapters 6, 7, 8. On changing views of Stresemann and his work, see Hans W. Gatzke, "Gustav Stresemann: A Bibliographical Article," *Journal of Modern History,* XXXVI (1964), 1-13.

since Bismarck had brought Prussia from Olmütz to Sedan.[53] This is perhaps an exaggeration—Stresemann himself, who in his last months saw only the incompleteness of his work, would probably have thought so[54]—but one has only to remember Germany's condition when he was capitulating to France in 1923 to be impressed by how much he had been able to build on that original act of necessity.

III

In July 1930, writing immediately after the final withdrawal of French troops from the Rhineland, and addressing himself particularly to the possibility of Franco-German collaboration in the future, the British ambassador in Paris wrote:[55]

> If the Germans create the impression here that they do not appreciate the spirit of [the French withdrawal] and merely use it as a peg on which to hang fresh demands, they will play into the hands of M. Briand's critics . . . The advice, therefore, to Germany is that in her own interest she had better go slow now and rest content for the present with what Stresemann's enlightened policy has already achieved for her.

These were wise words. If the iron law of necessity had compelled Rathenau in 1920 and Stresemann in 1923 to bow to French demands, it was still a necessity—or at the very least a counsel of prudence—for Germany to consult French wishes and avoid offending French susceptibilities in 1930, especially in view of the deepening economic misery of Germany and the possibility that out of French friendship might come some measure of relief. But this advice was lost on the man who now directed German affairs, Heinrich Bruening.

[53] Bainville, quoted in Godfrey Scheele, *The Weimar Republic* (London, 1946), p. 247.
[54] See his interview with Bruce Lockhart, reported in *Retreat from Glory*, pp. 338 ff.
[55] *Documents on British Foreign Policy, 1919-1939*, edited by E. L. Woodward and R. D. Butler (London, 1946 ff.) [hereafter cited as *British Documents*], 2nd series, I, 479.

Like Kiderlen-Wächter, Bruening has been accorded a degree of respect by writers on German affairs that is out of all proportion to his accomplishments. That he was an honorable man with a deep love of his country, that he was a courageous man who never faltered in his determination to solve her difficulties, and that the problems with which he had to deal were perplexing, must be admitted. But this should not obscure the fact that he was a headstrong and willful statesman who believed that action was always better than inaction, even if it was taken without reflection,[56] and whose tactics in foreign affairs did not bring advantage to his country.

Bruening's willfulness was demonstrated also in the domestic sphere, where, in the opinion of qualified observers, he created, or at the very least aggravated, his own difficulties. Called to the head of the government in March 1930, he was determined to brook no interference or delay on the part of the Reichstag as he put his program into effect; and he favored government by decree before that expedient had proved to be necessary. His mind was closed to the possibilities of compromise within the existing parliamentary system and impervious to warnings of the probably unhappy consequences of dissolving parliament in the midst of a severe economic depression.[57] He brushed the doubters aside and forced the dissolution of July and the elections of September 1930; and this brought 107 Nazis into the Reichstag and confronted him with an almost impossible situation. To master it, he decided to rely—as Bismarck

[56] In his book *The War and German Society* (New Haven, 1937), A. Mendelssohn-Bartholdy writes of the rise during the First World War of "a new philosophy of public morals called decisionism. It denounced caution as unmanly. It upheld the virtue of courage in taking the responsibility for the rights and wrongs of an ill-considered decision on the ground that actually *taking* it, either this way or that, even if it proved wrong or unnecessarily expensive, is always better than shrinking from responsibilities and losing Fortune's fleeting moment. . . . The emergency decrees of 1931 were officially justified by the President and his Cabinet almost in the same words as those used by the Imperial Government in 1914 and 1918. In his radio address to the German people on August 4, 1931, Chancellor Bruening confessed that some of the measures taken by the Government during the three preceding weeks . . . might have proved ineffective . . . but, the point was, the Government had had to *act* at any cost." (p. 41.)

[57] K. D. Bracher, *Die Auflösung der Weimarer Republik: Eine Studie zum Problem des Machtverfalls in der Demokratie* (2. Aufl., Stuttgart, 1957), p. 338 and note.

had done when he was breaking the opposition of the Prussian parliament in the 1860's—upon victories abroad. But the tactics he chose were hardly designed to repeat the great Chancellor's success. Even before the elections, Bruening had begun to use the French concession in the Rhineland as a peg on which to hang fresh demands. The French troops were hardly past the border before the German government was raising its voice to demand the evacuation of the Saar as well. The manifesto that hailed the evacuation said bluntly, "Our brothers in the Saar still await the day of their return to the mother country";[58] and this was constantly reiterated in the months that followed. At the same time, there were indications that the Bruening government wanted to proceed at once with a revision of the eastern frontiers as well. As early as 3 July 1930, Bruening's Foreign Minister, Julius Curtius, was telling the British ambassador that "Germany could not rest content with her present frontier in the east";[59] and on 10 August Treviranus, a cabinet minister, made a provocative reference to the eastern frontiers in a public speech. He was reported to have said:

Now the east demands the unification of all German people. In the depths of our souls we are thinking of the truncated Vistula lands, of the unhealed wounds in the eastern flank, that withered lung of the Reich. We think of how outrageously Wilson was pressured into the unnatural cutting-off of East Prussia and of the halfbreed condition to which Danzig was condemned. The future of our Polish neighbors, who owe their power as a State not the least to sacrifices of German blood, can only be assured if Germany and Poland are not kept in a condition of unrest through an unjust demarcation of frontiers.[60]

This was more than a demand for peaceful revision. Its tone bordered on the menacing; and the Poles and their French ally were, not unnaturally, incensed. Treviranus chose to be surprised by the uproar over his speech, reacting, the British ambassador wrote, very much as William II used to react to protests against his not infrequent outbursts;[61] but his air of outraged innocence was not very convincing. Even the British—who tended to be more tolerant of

[58] *British Documents*, 2nd series, I, 488.
[59] *Ibid.*, p. 490.
[60] *Ibid.*, pp. 491 f. *Schulthess' Europäischer Geschichtskalender 1930* (München, 1931), p. 189.
[61] *British Documents*, 2nd series, I, 496.

Bruening's lapses than others—were disturbed; and Sir Robert Vansit-
tart wrote a cabinet memorandum warning against Germany's tactics
and intimating that the Bruening foreign policy offensive seemed to
forecast the raising of other touchy issues, including the old question of *Anschluss*.[62]

This was a sound guess. If Bruening and his colleagues were
young men in a hurry before the September elections, they were
even more so after. It seemed absolutely necessary now to win a
triumph abroad great enough to restore the government's prestige
after its electoral defeat;[63] and their search for an issue on which to
win one alarmed foreign opinion. A month after the elections, an
official in the British Foreign Office wrote to the Berlin embassy:
"We have recently been struck by the sudden . . . unexpected
emergence of a demand in Germany for the abolition of the de-
militarisation restrictions in the Rhineland," and he pointed out
that a member of the Bruening government had said publicly that
"the Rhineland was not really free owing to its being subject to
certain servitudes."[64] This appeared to indicate a desire to strike at
a basic part of the Versailles Treaty structure and to destroy the
very foundations of the Locarno settlement.

This issue was not, as a matter of fact, pursued further by the
Bruening government. Instead, as the depression deepened, they
belabored the Western powers with complaints and demands, urging
a further scaling down of reparations in the form of a revision of
the Young Plan, at the very moment when they were announcing,
rather ostentatiously, their intention of proceeding with the construction of a new "pocket battleship."[65] Both the French and the British
found a certain inconsistency in the position of a government that
pleaded poverty one moment and increased its military expenditures
the next;[66] but Bruening answered these criticisms with an argument

[62] *Ibid.*, p. 501, note.
[63] See, for instance, Julius Curtius, *Sechs Jahre Minister der deutschen
Republik* (Heidelberg, 1948), p. 361.
[64] *British Documents*, 2nd series, I, 517.
[65] This was the second of two ships the Germans were authorized to build.
The construction of the first had led to a long parliamentary battle in the
autumn of 1928. See Cuno Horkenbach, *Das deutsche Reich von 1918 bis
heute* (Berlin, 1930), pp. 255-258, 260, 262, 273, 278.
[66] See *British Documents*, 2nd series, II, 104, 115, 116, 124, 148 f., 207 f.;
Foreign Relations of the United States, 1931, I, 97 f., 108, 130 f.

that rapidly became the standard reply to all complaints: namely, that to sacrifice the ship (or, indeed, to show any evidence whatsoever of a conciliatory temperament) would be to give new ammunition to the extremist parties and to increase the possibility of revolution from the right. Thus, in July 1931, Bruening told the American ambassador Sackett that he

> was convinced that any public statement made by the Government which implied any renunciation of the meager rights granted by the Treaty of Versailles to Germany to build cruisers as replacements for the over-age ships which are now part of the German Navy would have so great a 'symbolic' meaning for the German nation that it would revive all the antagonisms and passions that had been allayed with some difficulty last spring at the time of the Reichstag debates on the subject. Even though this is principally a naval question, the younger army officers in particular would view this as so great a renunciation of the interests of the armed forces of Germany that the loyalty of the army would be heavily jeopardized. Brüning feels that notwithstanding the desperate financial condition of the country it is his obligation to safeguard the one arm of defense that is available for his use in controlling imminent disturbances, and that he has neither the strength nor the ability to risk sacrificing that protection— an eventuality which he knows, from his acquaintance with the serious internal political situation, would result if he issued [such] a statement . . .

There was a good deal of truth in this, of course, but Bruening's constant repetition of this argument, and his apparent assumption that his domestic difficulties freed him of the necessity of showing any consideration for the interests and the concern of other powers, annoyed the governments with which he dealt and on occasion made them doubt his sincerity.[67]

[67] *Foreign Relations of the U. S.,* 1931, I, 130-31. The suspicion was not entirely unjustified, for Bruening did use his domestic troubles as a kind of delicate blackmail. Years later, in a speech before the Rhine-Ruhr Club in Düsseldorf in June 1954, he was reported to have said: "If a government finds itself in difficult negotiations with foreign powers, it can be thankful if it is criticized sharply by the Opposition. In certain cases, a clever government requests penetrating criticism from the Opposition, in order to strengthen its own negotiating position *vis-à-vis* the foreign powers." Quoted in Bracher, *Auflösung,* p. 398, note 141.

So many writers have praised Bruening's gallant attempt to stave off National Socialism that it is easy to lose sight of the fact that his foreign policy, even if judged by the purposes that guided it, was remarkably maladroit. His condoning of menacing speeches about the Corridor and the Rhineland, his demand for a reopening of the Saar question, his stubborn insistence on the right to build his new *Panzerkreuzer,* alarmed Germany's neighbors without improving his domestic situation. The net result of all these frantic maneuvers was to make the French reluctant to grant concessions of any kind to Germany. Thus, at a time when some easing of reparations might have strengthened the Bruening government, such relief was postponed for months because of French stubbornness. The potential curative effects of the Hoover moratorium were certainly lessened by the delay in putting it into operation;[68] and the cause of the delay can be traced back to Bruening's tactics.

Basically his error was that he persistently underestimated the key position held by France in European affairs. It may be that he allowed himself to be misled by the sympathy he found in London and came to believe that he could effect a working Anglo-German combination to exact concessions from France. If so, he overlooked the fact that he possessed neither the political nor the economic resources necessary to make this kind of old-fashioned power policy work or to impress the British sufficiently to make them want to play his game. Any illusions he had in this respect should have been dispelled by the way in which the British came down on the French side during the controversy over the Austro-German customs union proposal of 1931.

The attempt to establish the *Zollunion* was the most serious diplomatic blunder committed by the Bruening government, and its effects were so widespread and so uniformly unhappy that Herbert Hoover, in his memoirs, has compared the Austro-German action with the murder at Sarajevo in 1914.[69] It is doubtful whether the projected customs union could ever, by the most ingenious legal casuistry, have been squared with the provisions of the Peace Treaty and the Geneva Protocol of 1922, although it is theoretically possible

[68] On the negotiations over this, see the pertinent papers in the volumes cited in note 66 of this chapter.

[69] *The Memoirs of Herbert Hoover,* III. *The Great Depression, 1929-1941* (New York, 1952), p. 62.

that the legal obstacles could have been removed by negotiation. But the striking feature of the joint announcement of the scheme was that it had not been preceded by the kind of diplomatic soundings that Stresemann had always employed; nor had any attempt been made to consult the French or the League of Nations.[70]

This was deliberate rather than the result of inadvertance, and Edward Bennett is probably correct in his suggestion that it was inspired by the feeling that "the only kind of foreign policy that was likely to win acclaim in Germany was one that wrested successes from a reluctant world" and that it would consequently be best to avoid "contaminating the Austro-German scheme with foreign support."[71] What seemed to be called for, in short, was a forcing play *à la mode de* Kiderlen-Wächter. But to be successful this would have required unity of will and tactics on the part of the two associates, and this proved to be conspicuous by its absence. What consultation there was between Berlin and Vienna was ineffective, and faulty coordination led to a premature disclosure of the plan before the partners were agreed about how to proceed once this had happened. When the international storm burst over their heads, the Austrian government seemed embarrassed about the whole business, while the German justification of the project struck many Europeans as disingenuous. The Bruening government argued that the *Zollunion* was intended as a contribution to the efforts currently being made by the Commission of Inquiry for European Unity to implement Aristide Briand's pan-European proposals of September 1929, and further described the scheme as a practical step toward the removal of tariff barriers and the revival of world trade. This was all a bit too elaborate to be sincere, particularly in view of the fact that the plan was being presented subtly to the German people as a first step towards *Anschluss* with Austria; and it increased rather than alleviated the suspicions of Germany's neighbors and contributed in the end to the defeat of the project.[72]

[70] Bracher, *Auflösung*, p. 400.

[71] Edward W. Bennett, *Germany and the Diplomacy of the Financial Crisis, 1931* (Cambridge, Mass., 1962), p. 309; Oswald Hauser, "Der Plan einer Deutsch-Oesterreichischen Zollunion und die europäische Föderation," *Historische Zeitschrift*, CLXXIX (1955), especially 57-65.

[72] Bennett, *Diplomacy of the Financial Crisis*, pp. 53, 78 ff.; Hauser, *loc. cit.*, pp. 65 ff., 73 ff.

It is now pretty well agreed that this exercise in diplomatic improvisation did not spring from Bruening's brain. Curtius and the Austrian vice-chancellor Schober played the leading roles in formulating it, and State Secretary von Bülow and Karl Ritter, chief of the Economics Department of the German Foreign Ministry, were deeply involved.[73] Bruening himself was more interested in the possibility of reparations revision than in the *Zollunion* and seems to have felt some uneasiness about the plan when it was first broached. The salient point, however, is that he was the head of the government, that he authorized the project, without seriously weighing the difficulties that would be raised by it, and that he subsequently defended it in the same way that he upheld all of his strokes of policy, with a complete failure to understand why the other powers had any grounds for complaint. "Germany had few rights," he told the British ambassador, "and if she were going to be checked at every turn, the position of his government would become untenable. Her right to enter into a customs union with Austria could not be disputed."[74] There can be no doubt, therefore, that Bruening must bear the responsibility for the subsequent protests and pressure of the powers, for the rejection of the customs union scheme at The Hague, for the loss of domestic prestige caused by this necessary retreat, for the catastrophic economic repercussions, and for the deepening of French suspicions that found its expression in the fruitless disarmament talks that preceded Bruening's fall from power in 1932.

IV

Making a virtue of necessity is a diplomatic art that requires not only courage, but also imagination, prudence, and great steadiness.

[73] It has been suggested that Bülow inspired the project, but there is no agreement. See, *inter alia,* the first chapters of Jürgen Geyl, *Austria, Germany and the Anschluss, 1931-38* (New York, 1963); F. G. Stambrook, "The German-Austrian Customs Union Project of 1931: A Study of German Methods and Motives," *Journal of Central European Affairs,* XXI (1961), 24-40; Curtius, *Sechs Jahre,* pp. 188 ff.; Bonn, *Wandering Scholar,* pp. 315 ff.; Eyck, *Geschichte,* II, 379 ff.; Bennett, *Diplomacy of the Financial Crisis,* pp. 44 ff.; *British Documents,* 2nd series, II, nos. 15, 28.

[74] *British Documents,* 2nd series, II, no. 8.

Walther Rathenau and Gustav Stresemann—the latter to a higher
degree than his predecessor—possessed these qualities, and because
they did, were able to turn even the weaknesses of their country
into a diplomatic asset. Heinrich Bruening had courage without the
qualities needed to temper it; and, defying the necessities of his
situation, he allowed his reckless energy to ruin the cause he served.

chapter four

THE AMBASSADOR AND HIS PROBLEMS
from Bismarck to Hitler

IN JUNE 1859 the Prussian minister to St. Petersburg, Otto von Bismarck, wrote to a friend that he understood that he was being accused in Berlin of playing politics on his own in Russia. He denied the charge, but went on to say, "If nevertheless I wanted to carry on independent political activity here, it would not be surprising if I should become involved in courses which [might seem in Berlin to be] mistaken, for I lack even the suggestion of an instruction . . . and I could be subjected to every kind of torture without being able to betray what our real intentions are."[1]

How many envoys serving abroad have echoed that complaint in the hundred years since it was written! The claim that their Foreign Office is mistreating them either by keeping them inadequately informed, or by paying no attention to their reports or their advice about policy, or by restricting their privileges and powers, or by countenancing practices that make it difficult for them to perform their duties, recurs with monotonous regularity in the private and the official correspondence of diplomats of the modern period. But the fact that it is so common should not lead us to dismiss it as a professional *idée fixe;* nor should our talent for finding explanations for everything in political, social, and technological change persuade us that we are confronted here with a decline of diplomacy made inevitable by the rise of democracy and the revolution in communi-

---

[1] *Gesammelte Werke,* xiv/1, 527.

cations and that, since it is inevitable, it need no longer engage our attention. Whatever truth there may be in these judgments, it is undeniable that, as long as the great powers continue to use the ambassadorial system, the efficiency of their policy will depend to some extent upon how well they use it; and, this being so, their methods, and the complaints of their agents, will continue to merit scholarly investigation.

In a consideration of the course of German foreign policy from Bismarck to Hitler, therefore, something may be gained from a study of the role and the problems of the ambassadors and other diplomats serving in the field.

I

The determination with which Bismarck set out to correct the disorder and lack of system that prevailed in the Prussian foreign service in 1862 has been mentioned above.[2] Here we can only note that it was successful in its results: that within a decade Bismarck had removed the worst of the abuses, improved the quality of the nation's representation abroad, and made the diplomatic service as effective an instrument of state policy as any in Europe. Certainly any of the major powers would have been glad to be served by the great Bismarckian envoys of the 1870's and 1880's: Hohenlohe, a delicate and ingratiating talent who succeeded in making the best of a very difficult position in republican France; Prince Henry VII of Reuss, member of an ancient Thuringian family, who received his diplomatic training in the lesser German courts and rose to full stature in St. Petersburg and Vienna;[3] Schweinitz, "the mighty Magus of the north,"[4] who succeeded Reuss in St. Petersburg and, in his blunt, soldierly way, quickly won the confidence of the Russian court; Radowitz, an energetic representative and a skilled negotiator who proved his abilities at the Congress of Berlin and who ended his career, years later, at the Algeciras conference; Münster, a Hanoverian nobleman, placid, easy-going, and with a strong sense of humor, a brilliant *causeur* who served long years in London and

---

[2] See above, Chapter One, pp. 4-5.
[3] See, for instance, Brauer, *Im Dienste Bismarcks*, p. 46.
[4] *Holstein Papers*, II, 53 ff.

Paris;[5] and Hatzfeldt, a man of somewhat irregular private life and with a strong dislike for routine and administration, but one who in his London years showed great skill in handling political questions and an almost intuitive ability to establish rapport with those with whom he had to deal.[6] And, in addition to these "great prophets,"[7] there were scores of less distinguished but nonetheless competent and devoted diplomats in other embassies and legations.

Bismarck chose his envoys with care and with an eye to their intelligence, their technical skills,[8] and their judgment; he lavished attention upon the most minute aspects of their conduct of business in order to train them for their tasks,[9] he protected their rights and privileges against attacks from outsiders and always sought to improve the material conditions in which they had to work;[10] and he always regarded them as the principal instruments by which his foreign policy was executed. Yet despite all this, and the fact that, from his own long experience in the field, he understood the problems and the feelings of envoys better than many foreign ministers have been able to do, Bismarck did not always make the most of the talent at his disposal, and his attitude towards his foreign service was responsible for some of the weaknesses of his system.

This was partly due to the excessive emphasis that he came to place upon the quality of discipline. Bismarck insisted that his ambassadors be men who would carry out their instructions loyally, accurately, and without undue argument. He came to place such importance on this that he actually said in a Reichstag debate in

[5] Münster was so easy-going that Herbert von Bismarck accused him of never reading any instructions that came into the embassy while he was on leave. Wolfgang Windelband, *Bismarck und die europäischen Grossmächte, 1879-1885* (Essen, 1940), p. 689, note 78. See also *Holstein Papers*, II, 145; but compare Holborn in *Archiv für Politik und Geschichte*, v, 493 f., Trützschler von Falkenstein, "Kontroversen über die Politik Bismarcks im Jahre 1887," *ibid.*, VI, 276, and Lancken, *Dienstjahre*, pp. 31 f.

[6] Radowitz, *Aufzeichnungen*, I, 255; Busch, *Tagebuchblätter*, III, 191; Goldschmidt in *Preussische Jahrbücher*, CCXXXVI, 31.

[7] The phrase is Werthern's. See Holborn in *Archiv*, v, 469.

[8] Holstein said of Schweinitz that "his career was materially helped by his outstanding stylistic gifts, because Prince Bismarck, more than he himself realizes, judges people by their style." *Holstein Papers*, II, 53.

[9] See Craig in *Foreign Service Journal*, XXXIII (June, 1956), 28, 38.

[10] See, for instance, *Gesammelte Werke*, XI, 512 ff., for a typical speech in the Reichstag on the hardships and expense of foreign service.

1872 that "an envoy is only a vessel that attains its true value when
it is filled with the instructions of the sovereign";[11] and, when he
encountered willful and protracted disobedience, he could be absolutely ruthless in dealing with it.

In Bismarck's behalf, two points must be made here. His emphasis on discipline was, for one thing, a reflection of the absence
of that quality in the service he inherited. In the pre-Bismarck
period, channels of communication between the field and Berlin
were not clearly laid down, and legations and embassies did not always recognize that they were in any sense subordinate to the
Foreign Office; and these conditions persisted for some years after
Bismarck came to power. In the 1860's, for instance, he had trouble
with Count Usedom, his minister at the court of Florence, a man
who had an excessive regard for his own qualities and a disinclination to accept advice from Berlin,[12] and also with Count Robert von
der Goltz, the ambassador in Paris, who believed that Bismarck's
policy was misguided and who put difficulties in the way of its
execution;[13] and, in the first half of the 70's, he had to deal with the
thorny case of Harry Arnim, who sought, with greater persistence
and less honorable motives than Goltz, to promote a policy diametri-
cally opposed to that laid down in the Foreign Office. Bismarck was
certainly not unjustified in combating this sort of thing and in insisting, as he did in a famous letter to Goltz, that the country could
have only one foreign policy at a time and that "it must be the
one on which the Ministry and the King are agreed." "If you want
to overthrow it," he continued, "and thereby to overthrow the Ministry, then you will have to undertake that here [in Berlin] in
the parliament and the press, and at the head of an opposition
party."[14]

[11] Gesammelte Werke, xi, 271.
[12] On the Usedom case, see Max Duncker, Politische Briefwechsel aus
seinem Nachlass, edited by J. Schultze (Stuttgart, 1923), pp. 444 ff.; Albrecht
von Stosch, Denkwürdigkeiten, edited by Ulrich von Stosch (Stuttgart, 1904),
p. 152; "Freytags Briefe an Stosch," Deutsche Revue, xxxvii (3) (1912),
146 f.; Eyck, Bismarck, ii, 209 f.
[13] Holstein wrote of Goltz that he was always saying, "The man [Bismarck]
is wrecking my German program." Holstein Papers, i, 23. This is rather less
than fair to Goltz, as a reading of Herbert Rothfritz, Die Politik des preussischen Botschafters Grafen Robert von der Goltz (Berlin, 1934) will show.
[14] Gesammelte Werke, xiv/2, 660. From this point until the end of section 1

In the second place, it must always be remembered that Bismarck was hampered by certain awkward constitutional circumstances. He could not simply command his ambassadors to obey him. The theory that ambassadors were the agents of the prince retained its force in Germany; Bismarck's envoys had the privilege of reporting directly to the King-Emperor; and Prussian tradition held that their primary allegiance was to the sovereign rather than to the Foreign Minister or the Chancellor. If, therefore, an ambassador persisted in refusing to heed instructions, Bismarck was forced, in defense of his own position, to take the most extreme measures against him.

This is what happened in the case of Harry Arnim, when that ambitious envoy, intent on promoting the monarchical cause in France, not only ignored Bismarck's arguments concerning the folly of this course and his pleas for a united foreign policy, but actually carried his fight directly to the Emperor and sought to use his court influence to undermine the Chancellor's position. Lacking the power to dismiss Arnim without the Emperor's assent, and unable to secure this, Bismarck had to use methods that have rightly been described as unscrupulous—secret intimations to the French government that Arnim could not be trusted, persistent faultfinding and complaints to the Emperor about the Paris envoy, the sedulous dissemination of malicious rumors about his private affairs, and other practices designed, not merely to weaken the Emperor's regard for the ambassador, but to goad Arnim into an indiscretion so outrageous that he could be driven out of the service and out of politics as well. In the end, these tactics succeeded.[15]

They succeeded not only in getting rid of Arnim but in putting an end to such incidents of insubordination. After 1875 there were no more Arnim cases. The authority of the Foreign Office over the envoys was unchallenged; attempts to circumvent the Chancellor became unthinkable; and the efficiency with which German policy was executed increased.

Yet the results were not all good. Ambassadors are not, after all,

---

of this chapter, I have followed very closely the argument made on pp. 42 and 44 of my article in *Foreign Service Journal*, xxxiii (June, 1956) and, in part, have reproduced the text, while supplying the authorities not presented there.

[15] On the Arnim case, see Hartung in *Historische Zeitschrift*, clxxi, 47 ff.; Wertheimer in *Preussische Jahrbücher*, ccxxii, 117 ff.; Rich in *Journal of Modern History*, xxviii, 35 ff.

supposed merely to be yes-men, but to display initiative of their own; and a nation has a right to expect that its envoys will, if necessary, take upon themselves the responsibility for objecting to policies that strike them as being unsound. One of the results of the ruthless tactics used to destroy Arnim was to discourage this kind of initiative and responsibility; and there must have been many German representatives after 1875 who were terrified at the thought of Bismarck's displeasure. If even Radowitz could write in his memoirs: "To oppose the Bismarck of the 70's and 80's in any matter would have been unthinkable to me!"[16] what must not have been the mood of lesser men? Certainly representatives hoping for promotion must have been tempted to refrain from doing or writing anything that might arouse the choler of their chief in Berlin.

How many envoys yielded to that temptation, it is impossible to say. It is possibly true that the "great prophets"—as one of them told Lord Salisbury[17]—always retained their independence of judgment.[18] But, even in their case, there is evidence of some shriveling of initiative. Bismarck's shadow hung over them constantly; their subordination to him drained them of independent will; and they were never quite the same after 1890, when they no longer felt him standing behind them. Kurd von Schlözer admitted this when he wrote after the Chancellor's dismissal: "We German diplomats, who were merely modest executors of Bismarck's will at foreign courts, grew with him and felt ourselves strong in the service we performed for this greatest of statesmen and for our fatherland. It is different now that he is gone. We ... can no longer speak in the name of an overwhelming personality. . . ."[19]

An even graver deficiency in Bismarck's administration of his foreign service was his habit of doing what he had himself complained about in 1859, keeping his ambassadors in the dark concerning his intentions. Schweinitz once wrote that "in critical situations Bis-

[16] Radowitz, *Aufzeichnungen*, I, 266. See also Arthur von Brauer, "Die deutsche Diplomatie unter Bismarck," *Deutsche Revue*, XXXI (2) (1906), 69-78.

[17] Krausnick in *Historische Zeitschrift*, CLXVII, 566; *G.P.*, XIII, 24.

[18] For discussion of this, see H. Rothfels, "Die Erinnerungen des Botschafters Radowitz," *Archiv für Politik und Geschichte*, IV (1925), 389 f.; and Holborn, *ibid.*, V, 469 ff.

[19] Schlözer, *Letzte römische Briefe*, pp. 149 f.

marck loved to leave the chiefs of mission who were not directly involved without information. Thus, they could compromise themselves but not him."[20] Unfortunately, this practice was sometimes extended even to envoys in the heart of affairs. Ambassadors were likely to pursue a course of negotiation with energy and perseverance only to learn in the end—as Goltz did in the sixties[21]—that Bismarck had never really intended their negotiations to succeed. Chiefs of mission sometimes received reprimands for failure to carry out instructions that were, in fact, so cryptic as to be misleading. Much of the confusion that marked the Anglo-German talks with respect to Angra Pequena in 1884 was the result of Bismarck's failure to take his ambassador in London into his confidence; and this was no inadvertence on his part, for, when his State Secretary urged that more information be sent to Münster, Bismarck curtly rejected this as unnecessary.[22]

In such circumstances, it was easy for envoys to make mistakes. Even such an experienced hand as Reuss, the ambassador in Vienna, proved capable in 1887 of flying in the face of one of the fundamental axioms of Bismarck's diplomacy: his insistence that the alliance with Austria was a strictly defensive instrument. Inadequately informed, and bewildered by Bismarck's tactics, Reuss made the mistake of intimating to the Austrians that they would receive German support even if they precipitated a war—an interpretation which he had subsequently to correct.[23]

There is no more striking proof of the ill effects of Bismarck's refusal to introduce his ambassadors into the secrets of his over-all policy than the result of the debate over the renewal of the Rein-

---

[20] Schweinitz, *Denkwürdigkeiten*, I, 200.

[21] See for instance, the documents on Goltz's negotiations with Napoleon III in 1867 in *Auswärtige Politik Preussens: Diplomatische Aktenstücke* (herausgegeben von der Historischen Reichskommission, Oldenburg, 1931 ff.), VIII, *passim*.

[22] See William O. Aydelotte, "The First German Colony and its Diplomatic Consequences," *Cambridge Historical Journal*, V (1937), 302, 312. In face of this, the criticisms of Münster in W. L. Langer, *European Alliances and Alignments* (2nd ed., New York, 1950), pp. 294 f., Sontag, *Germany and England*, pp. 195 f., and Windelband, *Bismarck und die europäischen Grossmächte*, pp. 565, 620 seem to go too far. Cf. M. von Hagen, *Bismarck und England* (Stuttgart, 1941), p. 100.

[23] Krausnick, *Holsteins Geheimpolitik*, p. 155.

surance Treaty in 1890. One might have supposed that at least Bismarck's "great prophets" would defend the tie with Russia, which
was so indispensable a feature of his diplomacy. They did not do
so, or, for that matter, seem even to appreciate what was at stake.
Familiar only with the problems of their own posts, they were
imcompetent to judge the greater issues of policy.[24] Thus, at the
moment of crisis, Bismarck's faulty methods of dealing with his foreign service helped destroy the foundations of his diplomatic
system.

II

In the period that followed Bismarck's dismissal and extended to
the First World War, the chiefs of mission abroad lost prestige and
influence. Some men of energy and independence rose in these years
to positions of importance in the service; Monts, Bernstorff, Kühlmann, and Wolff-Metternich were all men of courage and integrity.
But even these few did not match their Bismarckian predecessors in
talent; and the great majority of the members of the diplomatic
service seem to have been competent but unremarkable servants of
the state. Tirpitz' gibe, to the effect that they were either "degenerate members of the high aristocracy or sons of big industrialists,
who were incapable of continuing their fathers' work,"[25] was doubtless unjustified, but it is perhaps not insignificant that it could be
made.

In many cases, diplomats in the field seem to have acquiesced in,
and almost to have invited, the reduction of their influence on
policy. The power exercised by Holstein after 1890 was hardly
calculated to encourage independence of thought in the embassies,
especially after it became clear that he was systematically rooting
out Bismarckian or supposedly Bismarckian envoys.[26] In addition to
this, the difficulty of keeping up with internal shifts within the

[24] Hajo Holborn, "Diplomats and Diplomacy in the Early Weimar Republic," in The Diplomats, p. 127. An exception might almost be made in
the case of Reuss. See G.P., VII, 36 and Erich Brandenburg, From Bismarck
to the World War (London, 1933), p. 32.

[25] Freiherr von Freytag-Loringhoven, Menschen und Dinge wie ich sie in
meinem Leben sah (Berlin, 1923), p. 146.

[26] Raschdau, Unter Bismarck und Caprivi, pp. 206 ff.

Foreign Office induced caution. "Today," wrote Monts, "a chief of mission never really knows who is cook and who is bottle-washer in Berlin." Because he didn't, it was just as well to play it safe and, as far as possible, to describe conditions at his post, "not as they actually are but as people in Berlin wish to seem them."[27] Diplomats might complain about this situation;[28] but they very rarely attempted to defy it. "I heard it said recently," wrote the court chamberlain, Zedlitz, "that Herr von Flotow, who was embassy counsellor in Paris during the Morocco affair, was complaining that he could never write and tell how the Moroccan business really stood, but only how the Foreign Office in Berlin would really have it."[29] This was an all too typical remark.

But the reduction of the influence that envoys in the field had on policy was also caused by a development that began in 1883, when the General Staff became an independent agency and began to demand reports from staff officers attached to the legations and embassies abroad. It was inevitable that the reports of these military, and later naval, attachés should begin to deal with political as well as military matters and that their political opinions should often contradict those expressed in the regular diplomatic dispatches; and it was natural, given the international atmosphere after 1900 and William II's penchant for the military, that the reports of the attachés should receive more attention in Berlin that the diplomatic ones.[30]

There is no more melancholy reading than the dispatches that the ambassador Wolff-Metternich wrote from London between 1901 and 1912, seeking to convince authorities at home that a naval accommodation between Britain and Germany was absolutely essential if war was to be avoided. In June 1909, for instance, Metternich wrote:

> I am perfectly well aware that my position in the fleet question—where I have, in accordance with my duty, repeatedly indicated that our re-

---

[27] Monts, *Erinnerungen*, p. 49.

[28] See Gustav Graf von Lambsdorff, *Die Militärbevollmächtigten Kaiser Wilhelms II. am Zarenhofe, 1904-1914* (Berlin, 1937), p. 28.

[29] Graf Zedlitz-Trützschler, *Zwölf Jahre am deutschen Kaiserhof* (Berlin, 1924), p. 199.

[30] On this, see Gordon A. Craig, "Military Diplomats in the Prussian and German Service: The Attachés, 1816-1914," *Political Science Quarterly*, LXIV (1949), 65-94.

lations with England are poisoned principally by it—is not applauded by His Majesty; and that the State Secretary of the Imperial Office of the Navy in particular [Tirpitz] attacks my position before His Majesty. It is naturally not pleasant for the naval leadership to hear that our rate of construction and our good relations with England stand in inverse proportion. But I would be falsifying history if I reported otherwise than I do, and I cannot sell my convictions, even for the favor of my sovereign. It is doubtful in any case whether His Majesty would be well served by a placid and ingratiating kind of reporting until the moment when we suddenly found ourselves at war with England.[31]

Unfortunately, every attempt made by Metternich to show his royal master the truth was counteracted by the reports of his naval attachés; and, in the end, William II—acting out of the conviction that Metternich was "too flabby," "absolutely unteachable in naval questions," and "hopelessly incurable"—removed him from his post.[32] The incident by itself tells the whole story of the ineffective role played by the ambassadors in the Wilhelmine period.

III

With the establishment of the republic, at least one noticeable change took place; and this was an exceptional flowering of new talent in the German diplomatic service. The conservative and aristocratic social strata from which the service was traditionally recruited now supplied such outstanding representatives as Leopold von Hoesch, ambassador in Paris from 1923 to 1932 and in London from that date until 1936, Dr. Wilhelm Solf, who performed eight years of distinguished service in Tokyo, and—among the younger men—Rudolf Nadolny, first ambassador of the republic to Turkey, Ulrich von Hassel, later to be ambassador in Rome, and Wipert von Blücher, who was to occupy the legation in Helsinki under Hitler. From the same class came that great original who deserves in every

---

[31] G.P., xxviii, 167.
[32] See Woodward, *Great Britain and the German Navy*, pp. 172 ff.; Wilhelm Widenmann, *Marine-Attaché an der kaiserlich-deutschen Botschaft in London, 1907-1912* (Göttingen, 1952), pp. 276 ff.; Richard von Kühlmann, *Erinnerungen* (Heidelberg, 1948), pp. 293 ff.

way to be ranked with Bismarck's ambassadors, Ulrich Count Brockdorff-Rantzau, the first republican ambassador to the Soviet Union, a
thin, wraithlike figure who might have stepped from the pages of
one of Hoffmann's tales, and who impressed the Communists as
much by the aristocratic hauteur of his mien as by his fierce conviction that Germany and the Soviet Union were fated to be partners against the West.[33] Simultaneously, new men came from the
ranks of politics to fill posts abroad, the most distinguished, perhaps,
being the former mayor of Hamburg, Friedrich Sthamer, who served
in London from 1920 until 1929; while others came from journalism,
like the three socialists who became successful envoys: Adolf
Müller, who served at Berne from 1920 to 1933; Ulrich Rauscher,
who was chief of mission in Warsaw from 1922 to 1930; and Adolf
Köster, who served first at Riga and later at Belgrade.[34]

This was an impressive group, and their services were notable.
Even if we grant—as we must grant—that the predominance of
economic questions and the pressing urgency of the military problem
created by the Versailles terms were turning whole areas of policy
over to financial experts or—as was true of much of Russian policy
—to soldiers,[35] and that this was restricting the traditional sphere of
action in which the diplomats had moved, it is nevertheless true that
effectiveness of German policy under Stresemann, for instance, must
be explained in part by the services of the men in the field. For
the gradual improvement of Franco-German relations after the Ruhr
invasion, Hoesch, whom even Poincaré admired, was to some degree
responsible; in preparing the way for Germany's entrance into the
League, Adolf Müller did important work;[36] and in promoting British
understanding of German objectives, Sthamer in London was almost

[33] Vallentin, *Stresemann*, pp. 198 f.; Dirksen, *Moskau, Tokio, London*,
p. 59; Herbert Helbig, "Die Moskauer Mission des Grafen Brockdorff-
Rantzau," *Forschungen zur Osteuropäischen Geschichte*, II (1955).

[34] On all this, see Holborn in *The Diplomats*, pp. 151-52; W. von Blücher,
Rapallo, pp. 12, 42; Dirksen, *Moskau, Tokio, London*, pp. 29 f.

[35] See George W. F. Hallgarten, "General Hans von Seeckt and Russia,
1920-22," *Journal of Modern History*, XXI (1949); Gatzke, *Stresemann and
German Rearmament, passim*; and the authorities cited in Craig, *Politics of
the Prussian Army*, pp. 408-415.

[36] Holborn in *The Diplomats*, pp. 151 f.

as effective as his British opposite number in Berlin, Lord d'Aber-non.[37]

It is, however, also worth noting that the greatest achievements of the Weimar diplomats in the field were accomplished in the Strese-mann period. Indeed, by 1930, all of the envoys mentioned above, with the exception of Hoesch and Müller and the younger men, were either dead or in retirement; and they were, for the most part, replaced by less original spirits. Herbert von Dirksen, for instance, who succeeded to the Moscow post, was no second Brock-dorff,[38] and Sthamer's successor in London was Constantin von Neurath, a diplomat who had the reputation of lacking both energy and moral courage,[39] a reputation that he was to confirm during his latter years of service as Foreign Minister under Hitler.[40] In the period that followed, as a member of the German diplomatic corps has written, figures like Solf and Brockdorff, who, in addition to diplomatic experience and technical qualifications, possessed political insight and initiative, were conspicuous by their absence; and even the best minds in the service were men who spent their time in political analysis and reporting rather than in making policy proposals.[41]

This tendency was encouraged by a development that had become clear even in Stresemann's time: the tightening of the control of the Foreign Ministry over the envoys in the field. After a period of great confusion in the first postwar years, when projects of democratic control and plans of administrative reorganization had made the orderly pursuit of business difficult in Wilhelmstrasse, the professional diplomats had reasserted their influence; and questions of policy and also of appointment, promotion, and transfer fell increasingly under the control of the incumbents of the newly defined posts of State Secretary and Deputy Divisional Director [Dirigent] in the Foreign

[37] For an example of Stresemann's reliance on Sthamer, see Thimme in Historische Zeitschrift, CLXXXI, 324.

[38] On Dirksen, see Carl E. Schorske, "Two German Ambassadors," in The Diplomats, especially pp. 478-481.

[39] See André François-Poncet, Souvenirs d'une ambassade à Berlin (Paris, 1946), p. 49.

[40] See Gordon A. Craig, "The German Foreign Office from Neurath to Ribbentrop," in The Diplomats, pp. 408 f., 423.

[41] Rudolf Rahn, Ruheloses Leben (Düsseldorf, 1949), pp. 74 f.

Ministry.[42] In the mind of an envoy at a second-rate post, or an ambitious first secretary who desired a transfer to Berlin, the figures of the State Secretary and the *Dirigenten* bulked very large. Since he knew that his work was judged by them, he was likely to err on the side of caution and to be even more conservative and traditional than they were, quite rightly, reported to be.[43]

It was perhaps only natural that the German foreign service should be subject to the process of bureaucratization that has affected so much of the twentieth century's organized social activity. Had there been a strong tradition of individualism or a professional ethic that put a high evaluation upon personal initiative, this might not have been true; but these values had, as we have seen, been the subject of official disapproval as early as Bismarck's time and could no longer be expected to inspire the behavior of the majority of the diplomatic service in the days when Germany was passing under the control of Adolf Hitler.

IV

On 21 April 1938 Adolf Hitler and General Keitel discussed various contingencies which, if they occurred, could be exploited to justify a German attack upon Czechoslovakia. Of three specific cases that they considered, the third was one of "Lightning action based on an incident (for example, the murder of the German Minister in the course of an anti-German demonstration)."[44]

The record of this conversation does not, unfortunately, tell us whether this case was discussed in purely theoretical terms, or whether consideration was actually given to the possibility that the envoy in Prague—whose name, incidentally, was Eisenlohr and who was not a member of the Nazi party—might be sacrificed for reasons of state. In view of some of Hitler's other actions, we have no

[42] See Paul Seabury, *The Wilhelmstrasse* (New York, 1955), pp. 17 f.; Dirksen, *Moskau, Tokio, London,* pp. 29 ff., 54 ff.; W. von Blücher, *Rapallo,* pp. 52 f.; H. G. von Studnitz, "Gestalt und Aufbau des Auswärtigen Amtes," *Aussenpolitik,* III (1952), 794.

[43] On Carl von Schubert, Staatssekretär from 1924 to 1930, see Holborn in *The Diplomats,* p. 154; on Bülow, Staatssekretär from 1930 until 1936, see Craig, *ibid.,* pp. 407 f., and François-Poncet, *Souvenirs,* pp. 240 f.

[44] *German Documents,* series D, II, 239.

very good reason for supposing that his conscience would have hesitated over this; and his opinion of diplomats was so low, in any case, that it bordered on contempt.

It should be noted at least parenthetically that Hitler himself possessed diplomatic gifts of the first order. He was always able to sort out the diverse elements of a complicated situation and seize upon the salient point; he never forgot the supreme importance of maintaining the initiative in ongoing political discussions; he had an intuitive sense for the tensions affecting others and was skilful in the exploitation of their hopes and fears; and he showed real virtuosity in the use of public diplomacy—that is, in the employment of the various instruments and techniques of the mass media of communication—in international intercourse. In this last respect, his masterful Peace Speech, delivered before the Reichstag on 17 May 1933 and the statement which he made in an interview with Ward Price of the London *Daily Mail* four days after his abrupt withdrawal from the Disarmament Conference and the League of Nations in October of the same year deserve study as models of the way in which the public statement can be used to divide and dissipate potential opposition.[45]

In intimate negotiation, the very heart of classical diplomacy, Hitler was also talented. Of his talks with Sir John Simon and Anthony Eden in March 1935, during which he not only allayed the alarm caused by his recent repudiation of the arms clauses of the Versailles Treaty but further prepared the way for the Anglo-German Naval Accord of June, the interpreter Paul Schmidt, who had served Stresemann, wrote later: "In all of the negotiations with the Englishmen, I found him a man who, with skill, intelligence and full recognition of the forms to which I was accustomed in political talks of this kind, presented his point of view as if he had done nothing for years except take part in such conversations. The only thing that was a departure from the customary was the length of his expositions. . . . The loudness of his voice never exceeded that which I have heard in the more excited phrases of other

[45] *The Speeches of Adolf Hitler*, edited by Norman H. Baynes (Oxford, 1942), II, 1041-1058; Alan Bullock, *Hitler: A Study in Tyranny* (revised edition, New York, 1962; Harper Torchbook edition, 1964), pp. 321-324; Hans Bernd Gisevius, *Adolf Hitler: Versuch einer Deutung* (München, 1963), p. 208.

international talks. Even his formulations were completely in accord with custom. He expressed himself clearly and easily and was obviously very sure of himself and his case."[46]

As in the military field, however, where Hitler also possessed undeniable competence, he was reluctant to admit that others might also have knowledge or talents that deserved consideration, and he always resented the trained professionals.[47] He had a deep-seated aversion against the Foreign Office—which he called a *"Sammelsurium von Kreaturen"*[48]—and he regarded diplomats as effete parasites who lived easy lives abroad but did nothing to justify their privileges. Their "stupid dispatches" were obviously not worth reading, and it would perhaps be best to do away with them entirely or to use them only for the most innocuous forms of representation, as *Vergnügungsdirektoren.*[49] "Of what use were our diplomats to us? What did they teach us before the First World War? Nothing! During the First World War? Nothing! After the First World War? Nothing!"[50]

When Hitler took office in 1933, Germany's diplomats had, of course, no very precise understanding of any of his views and certainly no hint that he might consider them, even theoretically, as more useful to him dead than alive; and they did not hesitate long over the decision to serve him. Of the senior members of the diplomatic service only one had laid down his office. On 6 March 1933, the ambassador in Washington, Prittwitz, decided to resign, explaining in a dispatch written five days later that his political views were "rooted in the soil of a free form of government . . . and the basic principles of republican Germany."[51] The other chiefs of mission were persuaded without much difficulty that it was their duty as

[46] Paul Schmidt, *Statist auf diplomatischer Bühne, 1923-45* (Bonn, 1949), pp. 295 ff.

[47] See Percy Schramm's introduction to Henry Picker, *Hitlers Tischgespräche* (2nd edition, Stuttgart, 1963), pp. 81 f.

[48] J. C. Fest, *Das Gesicht des Dritten Reiches: Profile einer totalitären Herrschaft* (München, 1963), p. 247.

[49] Hermann Rauschning, *Gespräche mit Hitler* (Zürich, 1940), pp. 249 ff.; Picker, *Tischgespräche*, pp. 238, 349 f.

[50] *Hitler's Secret Conversations*, edited by H. R. Trevor-Roper (New York, 1953), p. 226.

[51] *German Documents*, series C, I, 147 f.

civil servants to remain at their posts;[52] and any doubts that survived the appeal to their bureaucratic loyalty were put to rest by State Secretary Bülow, who advised them to carry on and, who intimated confidently that, even under the Nazis, business would go on very much as usual.[53]

This, of course, was far from true, although some time passed before this was discovered. One of the first to learn how different the conduct of business was to be under the Nazis was Rudolf Nadolny. This energetic diplomat had been called from his post in Ankara by Bruening in 1931 and made head of the German delegation to the Disarmament Conference in Geneva, a post he still held when Hitler assumed power. Throughout 1933 he waged so skillful a fight for the principle of parity of armaments that he won the admiration even of his chief antagonists.[54] Yet, at the very moment when he seemed on the point of winning his campaign, Hitler withdrew abruptly from both the conference and the League of Nations, without consulting Nadolny's views;[55] and when he attempted to protest he was ordered to his new post in Moscow.[56] Here he soon discovered that, while he was expected to go through the motions of cultivating Soviet friendship, his government was in

[52] In the American edition of his book, Dirksen has written: "We felt it to be our duty to assist in the process of normalization. . . . It was not until years later that I heard of the earnest and insistent requests which had been made to this effect by Chancellor Bruening to Bülow. As to the constitutional and juridical implications of the new situation, the permanent officials were perfectly justified in placing their services at the disposal of the party which had gained power by constitutional and democratic elections." *Moscow, Tokyo, London: Twenty Years of German Foreign Policy* (Norman, Okla., 1952), p. 107. This does not appear in the German edition. See also Rahn, *Ruheloses Leben*, pp. 95 f., and Erich Kordt, *Nicht aus den Akten* (Stuttgart, 1950), pp. 51 f.

[53] See, for instance, *German Documents*, series C, 1, 21. Hoesch, probably under Bülow's influence, told Sir John Simon on 31 January that "these domestic changes do not betoken any change in the line of German foreign policy." *British Documents*, 2nd series, IV, 401.

[54] See, for instance, *German Documents*, series C, 1, 477.

[55] *Ibid.*, pp. 912 f., 922 ff.; *British Documents*, 2nd series, V, 694; Rudolf Nadolny, *Mein Beitrag* (Wiesbaden, 1955), pp. 140 f.; Artur W. Just, "R. Nadolny," *Aussenpolitik*, IV (1953), 385; Gerhard Meinck, *Hitler und die deutsche Aufrüstung, 1933-37* (Weisbaden, 1959), pp. 41 ff.

[56] See Hitler's account of the failure of Nadolny's attempt to enlist Hindenburg's support in Henry Picker, *Tischgespräche*, p. 369.

fact determined to break the connection that had been made twelve years before at Rapallo. Nadolny returned to Berlin to protest against this course, had an unsatisfactory series of meetings with Hitler, refused to go back to his post, and was dismissed.[57]

Other diplomats on mission were meanwhile learning the difficulties of carrying on normally under the new regime. It was now infinitely more difficult than it ever had been in the Wilhelmine age to tell who was cook and who was bottlewasher in Berlin; and the bewildering proliferation of party agencies made it hard for a chief of mission to understand the degree of respect owed to the dozens of uniformed and un-uniformed dignitaries from Germany who descended upon him.[58] The emergence of new units claiming competence in foreign affairs—the Rosenberg organization, the Ribbentrop bureau, and various economic agencies—also posed delicate problems to diplomats who did not wish to hurt their careers either by satisfying, or by refusing, requests made by these agencies. In addition, it soon became apparent that party allegiance was going to be a more perplexing problem than had originally been supposed. After 1933, the National Socialist party's Foreign Organization (*Auslandsorganisation* or AO) began to grow in influence, to develop a foreign service of its own, to send agents abroad to spread Nazi propaganda, to maintain contact with subversive elements, and to extend party discipline over German nationals. The activities of the AO caused embarrassment to resident embassy staffs, and the Foreign Office protested continually against them. But by 1936 this battle had been lost and, at the beginning of the next year, the AO was given jurisdiction over all Germans living abroad, while its chief, E. W. Bohle, received an independent post inside the Foreign Ministry from which he could actually pass upon the loyalty and the efficiency of all German diplomats.[59]

All this the diplomats themselves were willing to tolerate as long as they could continue to participate in German foreign policy. But it soon became apparent that Hitler was going to make foreign policy without much reference to their wishes or their advice; and that he was not even willing to read their reports.

[57] Rahn, *Ruheloses Leben,* pp. 83-84; Nadolny, *Mein Beitrag,* pp. 167-169.
[58] See, for instance, *German Documents,* series C, 1, 432 ff.
[59] On the AO, see Craig in *The Diplomats,* pp. 427-30 and the authorities cited.

Whatever judgment one may feel called upon to make on the growing bureaucratization of the diplomatic service, and, more particularly, on its members' decision to continue to serve Hitler long after they were aware of the nature of his regime and of his racial policies, it must be admitted that the quality of their reporting between 1933 and 1939 was high and that its content deserved more attention than it received. But is is also true that the tone of the reports from abroad, especially in the first months of National Socialist power, was hardly likely to please Hitler, for it was cautious to the point of complete pessimism. Taking their lead perhaps from State Secretary Bülow, who wrote that "the idea of German activity seems . . . wrong to me. . . . At the moment our position in the world is exceedingly bad,"[60] the chiefs of mission were uniformly opposed to a dynamic policy. In addition, the ambassador in Moscow warned them of the grave consequences of loosening the Russian connection,[61] the minister to Berne warned against meddling in Swiss affairs,[62] the ambassador to France and the minister to Warsaw saw the possibility of preventive war against Germany,[63] and the ambassador to Italy saw dangers on every side.[64]

This opposition to an active strategy in foreign affairs continued through the first years and deepened when Hitler's policy offensive began to develop in 1935 and 1936. In the latter year, for instance, Hoesch seems to have been alarmed by the risks involved in occupying the Rhineland and to have supported his military attaché's opinion that there was an even chance of war if troops were marched in.[65] This sort of thing strengthened Hitler's instinctive contempt for the diplomatic calling. The diplomatic reports of his first years, he said later, had been "miserable," always counseling that "we should do nothing. . . . One day the business had been so stupid that he had inquired of the gentlemen how anything would ever be done if we did nothing."[66]

Hitler's scorn for the diplomats was so strong that, when he wished

[60] *German Documents*, series C, 1, 689 f.
[61] *Ibid.*, p. 246.
[62] *Ibid.*, p. 684.
[63] *Ibid.*, pp. 137, 342 f.
[64] *Ibid.*, pp. 660 f.
[65] Freiherr Geyr von Schweppenburg, *Erinnerungen eines Militär-attachés: London, 1933-37* (Stuttgart, 1949), pp. 87-88.
[66] Picker, *Tischgespräche*, p. 396.

to accomplish anything in a foreign capital, he generally relied on some kind of a special mission; and his regular chiefs of mission were reduced to the mere role of representation.[67] Moreover, when the Fuehrer geared his machine for its big drive for European mastery, he brought to the Foreign Ministry a man whose contempt for the professional diplomats was as great as his own, Joachim von Ribbentrop.

Josef Goebbels once said of Ribbentrop that "he bought his name, married his money and swindled his way into his office." The first two charges are roughly correct, and, if the third is a bit strong, it is certainly true that Ribbentrop did not win his post by demonstrated competence but by an artful campaign of flattery and imitation that persuaded the Fuehrer in the end that "Ribbentrop is a genius." In the course of this, he absorbed all of Hitler's prejudices and, from the moment when he became Foreign Minister, he operated on the assumption that policy was a matter for the Fuehrer and himself alone, and that even the experts of the ministry he now headed should have no role in it.[68] As for the envoys abroad, they were all defeatists and were—as he told Bülow's successor as State Secretary, Ernst von Weizsäcker—"no good in any case."[69] Not only were they to have no share in policy, but Ribbentrop could not see why they need even be given accurate information *about* policy. In August 1938, as the Czechoslovakian affair moved toward crisis, Ribbentrop had a circular instruction prepared for transmission to all German missions abroad. After Weizsäcker had read it, he had to go to the Foreign Minister and tell him that

> the instruction is not suitable to convince our Missions. Our Heads of Missions would believe the thickly laid on arguments just as little as I do. Neither was intervention by the Western Powers to be discounted in a conflict with Czechoslovakia, nor was our armament

[67] W. Hubatsch, "Die deutsche Berufsdiplomatie im Kriege," *Aussenpolitik,* vi (1955), 170 f. For the activities of one of these special envoys, see Hermann Neubacher, *Sonderauftrag Südost, 1940-45* (2. Aufl., Göttingen, 1957).

[68] See, for instance, the testimony of Steengracht von Moyland in *Trials of the War Criminals before the Nuernberg Military Tribunals* (14 vols., Nuremberg, 1946 ff.), xiii, 25. In general, see the chapter "Joachim von Ribbentrop und die Degradierung der Diplomatie" in Fest, *Das Gesicht des Dritten Reiches,* pp. 241 ff.

[69] Ernst von Weizsäcker, *Erinnerungen* (München, 1950), p. 182.

relatively as strong as in 1914, nor had we a recipe for the decisive defeat of the British and French. . . . Herr von Ribbentrop might dictate to his Ambassadors how they should speak, but he should give up the attempt to make fools of them.[70]

A striking aspect of German diplomacy in the crisis years 1938 and 1939 is that, at very critical moments, chiefs of mission were ordered to concern themselves with trivialities or were actually sent away from their posts. In July and August 1939, much of the time of the German ambassador in France was given over, on Ribbentrop's personal orders, to a squalid quarrel with the French government because it had refused to give a visa to Otto Abetz.[71] At the same time, Ambassador von der Schulenburg in Moscow—already engaged in the conversations with Molotov that were, largely because of his negotiating abilities, to flower into the Nazi-Soviet pact—had to ask Weizsäcker to do everything he could to persuade Ribbentrop not to insist that he break off his talks in order to appear in uniform at the Nuremberg Parteitag.[72]

In the same month of August, Dirksen, the London ambassador, came home on leave and was informed that he was not to return to his post until he had seen the Foreign Minister and received special instructions. He soon discovered that it was impossible to see Ribbentrop and that no one was interested in anything he had to say about the country to which he was accredited and which might, at any moment, be involved in war with Germany.[73] In the same month, the ambassador to Poland, who was also on leave, was ordered by Ribbentrop to remain in Berlin, to have no contact with any Polish authority, and to refrain even from communicating with his embassy by telephone. Since war with Poland was a very real possibility, the ambassador was puzzled by this conduct, pointing out that "without him his Embassy could be regarded as a company with-

[70] *German Documents*, series D, II, 527.

[71] *Ibid.*, series D, VI, nos. 640, 658, 664, 690, 755, 767; and VII, nos. 22, 49, 65.

[72] *Ibid.*, VII, no. 61. Schulenburg was intrigued by Molotov and he wrote: "This strange man and difficult character has now grown accustomed to me and has, in conversation with me, in great measure abandoned his otherwise always evident reserve. Any new man would have to start from scratch." On Schulenburg's negotiating skill, see *ibid.*, VI, especially no. 648.

[73] *Ibid.*, VI, no. 674; VII, nos. 115, 130; and Schorske in *The Diplomats*, pp. 509-510.

out its company commander"[74]—a not altogether fortunate figure of speech. Even in retrospect, the reasoning behind this Hitler-Ribbentrop method of sending ambassadors on compulsory leave in moments of crisis is not clear; and one is left feeling that it was probably a compound of contempt for customary diplomatic procedures, and apprehension lest the diplomats, if left at their posts, might actually try to influence the course of events.[75]

One thing was certain, and that was that, even when they were privileged to remain at their posts and go about their business, no one of real authority in Berlin paid any attention to their reports. There were many able dispatches being written by German envoys in Western capitals in the last months before the outbreak of the Second World War in Europe[76]—dispatches that specifically warned against some of the illusions that were entertained in the Reichskanzlei and Berchtesgaden and Ribbentrop's various retreats—but neither Hitler nor Ribbentrop seems to have pondered them. Both seem to have relied on those secret sources of inspiration that enabled Ribbentrop to tell Ciano in August 1939 that "his information, but above all his psychological understanding of England, made him certain that any British intervention was out of the question" in the case of a Polish-German war.[77]

In view of what happened to Germany in the war that began when the English did in fact intervene in Poland's behalf, it is clear that the nation was not well served by this cavalier disregard of the warnings of its ambassadors. Hitler was perhaps justified in being critical of the extremely pessimistic tone of some of the dispatches sent home in 1933; but to have concluded, as he seems to have concluded, that all warnings written by diplomats were groundless was surely an act of folly. It appears, indeed, that the only diplomatic reports Hitler would read were those that confirmed his own prejudices and opinions. Like William II, he preferred—in Wolff-Metternich's phrase quoted above—"a placid and ingratiating kind of reporting."

It is significant in this respect that Hitler's favorite diplomats

---

[74] *German Documents*, series D, VII, nos. 2, 32, 82.

[75] Weizsäcker, *Erinnerungen*, p. 182.

[76] *German Documents*, series D, VI, nos. 35, 69, 379, 430, 481, 564.

[77] Ministero degli Affari Esteri, *I Documenti Diplomatici Italiani* (Rome, 1952 ff.), 8th series, XIII, nos. 1, 102, 108, 116.

were Hans Thomsen, the chargé d'affaires at Washington after Ambassador Dieckhoff went on permanent leave in November 1938,
and Lieutenant General von Bötticher, the military attaché at the
same post. These men, Hitler said in May 1942, were "diplomats
who could not be bluffed" and "the reports which they sent us must
be regarded as models of their kind, for they invariably gave us a
perfectly clear picture of the situation."[78] This high praise must be
qualified at the very outset by the reminder that it came from a
man whose ignorance of the United States was so profound that in
1943 he could still believe—apparently on the strength of the film
"The Grapes of Wrath"—that the entire agricultural population of
this country was in a state of incessant migration.[79] But it is nevertheless worth dwelling for a moment on Hitler's admiration of
Thomsen and Bötticher.

The point is that the reports of these men told Hitler precisely
what he wanted to hear about the United States. Ambassador Dieckhoff's reports had been filled with warnings about America's potential power and the necessity of avoiding conflict with her and, as
early as December 1937, he was writing home that the German
government should not delude itself about the strength of American
isolationism, since even the most inveterate foes of foreign entangle-
ments would swing quickly from isolationism to intervention if they
discovered "that their doctrinaire conception . . . benefits the foes of
liberalism and democracy."[80] This did not make for pleasant reading,
and Dieckhoff was soon—as he suspected—considered a bore in
Berlin.[81] The reports that Thomsen and Bötticher sent, after Dieckhoff's recall in November 1938, were quite different.

Although by no means entirely devoid of good sense and shrewd-
ness, their dispatches conveyed the general impression to Berlin that

[78] Picker, *Tischgespräche*, p. 353. Among foreign ambassadors Hitler admired Oshima of Japan, because he was and acted like a soldier, and François-
Poncet of France, who was always able to get him excellent chocolates from
Paris. *Ibid.*, pp. 427-429. In the case discussed above, one of the objects of his
admiration was a soldier and both of them, figuratively at least, sent him
sweets.

[79] See Felix Gilbert, ed., *Hitler Directs His War: The Secret Records of
His Daily Military Conferences* (New York, 1950), p. 24.

[80] *German Documents*, series D, I, no. 423. See also nos. 427, 444, 445,
447, 451; IV, nos. 499, 500, 501, 502.

[81] *Ibid.*, I, no. 445.

isolationism was more powerful than in fact it was and that the United States was neither technically nor morally strong enough to overcome the German superiority in armaments or to participate effectively in a war.[82] Thomsen's reports breathed contempt of the American people and were filled with references to their mental dullness, their ignorance of Europe, their "proneness to wild enthusiasm and emotionalism," and their susceptibility to British, Jewish, and Communist propaganda and the promises of demagogues.[83] Bötticher, who saw Freemasons and Jews exercising control over the executive branch of the government and even insinuating themselves into the highest staffs of the armed services,[84] was capable of swinging to the opposite extreme and finding enthusiasm in the United States for German military victories where none existed, writing that "more and more pictures are appearing in the papers showing the Fuehrer in the field. . . . The opinion of Senator Pittman, who described the Fuehrer as a genius, is gaining ground."[85]

Whatever illusions this misguided optimism may have aroused, Bötticher's more serious fault was his depreciation of the productive potential of the United States. He found it impossible to believe that this nation could ever become a real arsenal of democracy; and, on 4 April 1940, he wrote scornfully that "the assertion that the American aviation industry can achieve an annual production rate of about 30,000 to 40,000 planes by the end of the year does not become more credible by frequent repetition."[86] This was the sort of thing Hitler liked to hear, and it is no mere coincidence that, twelve days after Bötticher's report was dispatched from Washington, the Fuehrer was telling the Commander-in-Chief of the

---

[82] See Joachim Remak, "Hitlers Amerikapolitik" *Aussenpolitik*, VI (1955), 711 ff. Remak's remarks about Bötticher have been confirmed by the recent publication of some of his dispatches.

[83] *German Documents*, series D, VI, nos. 107, 403. For other aspects of his views about the United States, see *ibid.*, VIII, no. 315; IX, nos. 26, 31, 417, 422, 493; X, nos. 47, 108, 186, 187, 190, 195, 322, 362. Thomsen was realistic enough to recognize, once Hitler's campaign in the Low Countries was launched, that the tide of American opinion was turning irrevocably against Germany, and he occasionally said so in his reports. *Ibid.*, IX, no. 243.

[84] *Ibid.*, X, nos. 195, 288.

[85] *Ibid.*, IX, no. 254. See also no. 96 and, for Weizsäcker's objections to this kind of reporting and Thomsen's reply, nos. 141 and 163.

[86] *Ibid.*, IX, no. 45. See also no. 236.

Swedish Navy that "[the production] of America was the biggest swindle on earth. For him all this was simply a joke."[87]

It was a joke, however, that the German people did not find very funny after they had been made to pay for Hitler's inability to use the resources of diplomacy for anything but a prop to his own wishful thinking.

V

The problems of Germany's representatives abroad had steadily increased and their influence on policy had steadily declined in the hundred years that separated Bismarck's time from Hitler's. This was due partly to the increasing complexity of foreign relations, which destroyed the monopoly once enjoyed by the professional diplomat, partly to the growth of centralized control over the foreign service, which even in Bismarck's time was reducing the independence of the embassies, and partly to the tendency toward bureaucratic modes of thought and behavior in the foreign service itself.[88] But, if these things reduced the role of the ambassador, they did not eliminate it from the practice of foreign relations. The success of Germany's foreign policy, like that of other powers, depended to a large extent upon a proper understanding of the interests, objectives, intentions, and strength of other nations; and the trained diplomat in the field was still the best instrument for acquiring the information that could make such understanding possible. It is no accident that the two German regimes that willfully denied this, and preferred the counsel of soldiers or the secret promptings of intuition to the advice that their ablest envoys could provide, led Germany to war and overwhelming defeat.

[87] *Ibid.,* no. 127. At Nuremberg after the war, Dr. Karl Ritter, the leading economic expert in the Foreign Ministry during the war, roundly condemned Bötticher as a dangerously stupid official. Every report concerning American production which he sent to Berlin closed, according to Ritter, with the words "It's all bluff!"; and this view was constantly reiterated by Hitler and his intimates. *New York Times,* 8 November 1947, p. 7.

[88] For other reflections on these tendencies, see H. G. von Studnitz, "Gesandte und Geschickte," *Der Monat,* 10. Jahrg., Heft 112 (January, 1958).

chapter five

THE STATECRAFT OF

Konrad Adenauer

WHEN THOMAS MANN wrote his last great novel, he brought it to a close with a moving comparison of the Germany of Hitler's time with the torn and broken country that emerged from the war.

> At that time [he wrote] Germany, with her cheeks feverishly flushed, reeled drunkenly at the height of her empty triumphs. . . . Today, girt round with demons, a hand over one eye but staring with the other into horrors, she plunges from despair to deeper despair. When will she reach the bottom of the abyss? When, out of the ultimate hopelessness, will the light of hope dawn, a wonder that passes all belief?[1]

The questions posed here by the artist were answered more quickly than anyone dared to suppose in 1947, when *Doktor Faustus* was published. The bottom of the abyss was reached in the following year; the light of hope dawned soon thereafter; and, by 1950, newspaper writers, seeking to describe the remarkable economic recovery of Germany, had already made the term "the German wonder" threadbare with use. Nor was the economic renascence of the country alone remarkable. By 1950 also, Western Germany, although still subject to controls and disabilities as a result of defeat in the war, had become an important and active factor in international

---

[1] *Doktor Faustus: Das Leben des deutschen Tonsetzers Adrian Leverkühn, erzählt von einem Freunde* (Stockholm, 1947), p. 773.

affairs once more; and five years later it had regained its full sovereignty and had been accepted as a member of the North Atlantic Alliance with rights and privileges equal to those of its former adversaries.

This political recovery was the result of the statecraft of Konrad Adenauer; and it would be inappropriate to conclude a series of lectures on German foreign politics without some consideration of his work. This is true despite the fact that we do not yet possess the documentary materials that would be necessary to enable us even to describe the Chancellor's policies with accuracy and the additional fact that any judgments made of those policies today are at the mercy of future events. These considerations will counsel caution; but they should not be allowed to discourage a tentative appraisal of the achievement of a man who, when he retired in October 1963, had controlled German foreign policy for a longer period than either Gustav Stresemann or Adolf Hitler.

I

One of Adenauer's most outspoken critics, the late Karl Georg Pfleiderer, used to say scornfully that the Federal Chancellor had come to foreign policy for the first time at an age when Bismarck was being sent into retirement.[2] Factually at least, this statement is accurate. Konrad Adenauer entered politics in the year 1906, as a junior adjunct in the government of the city of Cologne; and he remained in the municipal administration until 1933, serving as Chief Mayor of that Rhineland city from 1917 until he was dismissed by the Nazis in the latter year, and returning to that post for a brief period under British occupation authorities in 1945. He was considered as a candidate for the position of Chancellor of the Republic in 1926, but nothing came of this; and, apart from his duties as President of the Prussian State Ministry in the last years before Hitler came to power, he had relatively little contact with any sphere of action that lay outside the confines of his city. As for foreign affairs, although—as will appear below—he held firm views during the Weimar period, he had no real connection with policy matters until after the collapse of 1945.

[2] *Der Spiegel* (Hamburg), 2 June 1954, p. 12.

Nevertheless, even a person who insists on the limits of Adenauer's experience can hardly fail to note, if he looks into the details of his municipal service, that the qualities that made him a good Chief Mayor were precisely those that later made him a successful international statesman.

It was in Cologne, for instance, that Adenauer first developed the gift of refusing to be cowed by disaster. He became chief of the city administration only eighteen months before the surrender and the revolution of 1918. In the days when the city was filled with discharged and rebellious soldiers, when its food supply was uncertain, and when the fate of the whole of the Rhineland was hanging in the balance, not many people dared make plans for the future. Yet Adenauer operated on the principle that "times of political catastrophe are especially suitable for new creative ventures"; and he initiated a whole series of projects, ranging from the construction of new harbor installations to the building of additions to the university, which seemed utterly unrealistic at the time, but which were in fact realized and which transformed Cologne from a city in decline into one of the most progressive municipalities in western Europe.[3]

At the same time, Adenauer showed that he possessed a talent that is of inestimable importance to politicians of all kinds and to those who are concerned with foreign policy not least of all. He learned to explain complicated issues in such a way as to convince the electorate that they understood them and to make them want to vote for his way of handling them. Demonstrated perhaps for the first time in his successful campaign after the First World War to transform the old fortification belt of Cologne into a park area, a campaign in which Adenauer had to arouse public opinion against powerful and persuasive private interests,[4] this ability was refined and perfected over the years and became the mainstay of Adenauer's diplomacy. In foreign policy debates after 1949, his opponents often accused him of resorting to the grossest kind of over-simplification in his search for public backing.[5] Yet, while there is doubtless some

[3] See Paul Weymar, *Konrad Adenauer, die autorisierte Biographie* (München, 1955), pp. 93 f.
[4] *Ibid.*, pp. 96-99.
[5] See, for instance, the account of Adenauer's 1957 election campaign in *Der Spiegel,* 11 September 1957, pp. 13-33.

substance to these charges,[6] they are surely insufficient to explain
the fact that Adenauer won a measure of electoral support for
foreign policy requirements much greater than that secured by the
most successful Weimar statesmen. Nor can this be attributed solely
to the difference in political climate between Weimar and Bonn. In
the last analysis, it was due to the Chancellor's gifts of political persuasion. On his eightieth birthday, one of the editors of the *Deutsche
Rundschau* wrote: "Since the people of Germany received their sovereignty thirty-six years ago, he is the first Chancellor who has fully
mastered the technique of legitimate power. . . . With Adenauer,
the civilian spirit of the German bourgeoisie has for the first time
attained political success by means of a great parliamentary majority."[7] In somewhat different words, one might say that Adenauer
was the first German statesman who was able to overcome the
unconscious tendency of his countrymen to believe that leaders could
only be taken seriously when they wore uniforms. His political
style—which was stern, earnest and patriarchal—convinced them that
the authority for which they longed could be found in a democratic
regime under his leadership, and they never seriously wavered in
that faith until his retirement.[8]

If Adenauer's ability to win popular backing was acquired during
his early career in Cologne, so were the rudiments of his negotiating
ability. One of his early associates has written of the way in which
he would win over municipal councilors and interest groups to his
views.

> His first principle [this official has written] was to make himself com-
> plete master of the subject under discussion. This enabled him to
> counter every objection raised by the opposition immediately and
> effectively. . . . His second rule was: do not interrupt your oppo-
> nent but let him speak until he has . . . advanced the whole store

[6] An example of oversimplification is his statement to the Bundestag in
March 1955 that "so long as we do not belong to NATO we are, in the case
of a hot war between Soviet Russia and the United States, the European
battlefield; and, if we are in the Atlantic Pact Organization, we are no longer
that battlefield." *Frankfurter Allgemeine Zeitung,* 17 March 1955, p. 4.

[7] *Deutsche Rundschau,* 82. Jahrgang (January, 1956), p. 27.

[8] See Robert Comte d'Harcourt, *Konrad Adenauer* (Paris, 1955), p. 111,
and Hermann Proebst, "Zu früh und zu spät," in *Die Ära Adenauer:
Einsichten und Ausblicke,* ed. by Janko Musulin (Frankfurt am Main,
1964), p. 153.

of his arguments and has nothing in reserve. . . . [He also believed that] "the most successful man in politics is he who can outsit the rest". . . . He often saw to it that council and committee meetings dragged on far into the night. When everyone was dog-tired from the endless pro and contra of debate, he would finally come out with his own motion or proposal, which to hazy and sleepy minds would then appear like a summary of their own views, and they would adopt it without further ado.[9]

One can recognize in this description some of the qualities that Adenauer put to use in negotiations with his fellow party members in the first days of the Christian Democratic Union, before his leadership was clearly established, in his service as President of the Parliamentary Council—where, incidentally, General Clay sensed in this still relatively unknown party politician "the quality of statesmanship"[10]—and later in his dealings with the Allied High Commissioners. One of them, the Frenchman François Poncet, wrote later, "The genius of Adenauer lay actually in his ability to inspire confidence in his *vis-à-vis*, . . ., and to convince him that he could be a useful partner. . . . At the beginning, he had no comprehensive knowledge of problems outside of Germany. This modest civilian, confined to the great city that he administered, had remained a provincial. He had not travelled and he knew no foreign languages. He taught himself and made the adjustment to the style and usages of international diplomacy, and did so with an elasticity remarkable in a man of his age, who was moreover supposed (quite wrongly) to be uncouth, severe and humorless."[11] Poncet and his colleagues soon learned that the outsider had a natural affinity for the arts of negotiation; and among the Commissioners the persistence with which he followed his objectives became legendary. At the time of the Petersberg agreement of 1949, for instance, Adenauer haggled for a full day over the wording of the final communiqué and, when all his demands for revision had finally been granted, the French High Commissioner sighed wearily: "It is a very hard task, making presents to the Germans. It is also a very thankless task."[12] Similarly, in the

[9] Weymar, *Adenauer,* p. 95.

[10] General Lucius D. Clay, *Decision in Germany* (New York, 1950), p. 412.

[11] Quoted in Franz Rodens, *Konrad Adenauer: Der Mensch und Politiker* (München, 1963), p. 98.

[12] Weymar, *Adenauer,* pp. 475 f.

discussions of the details of the 1952 treaties regulating the stationing of Allied forces in Germany, Adenauer wore down his fellow negotiators by his apparent willingness to discuss minute points indefinitely and by his incredible mulishness on important issues. The exasperated American representative, ceding one more point, is reported to have said: "All right, then. This is now the one hundred and twenty-second concession the Allies have made to the Germans."[13]

Even the Russians were not entirely unimpressed by these arts of negotiation, which were, after all, not dissimilar to their own. The Chancellor's trip to Moscow in September 1955 was not perhaps (for reasons touched on below) a diplomatic triumph, and it was marked by one ugly scene in which the German statesman was the subject of a flood of Khrushchevian invective;[14] but when it was over a journal that had generally been hostile to the Chancellor's policy expressed a grudging admiration for his behavior in Moscow.

> From the moment of their first meeting, the Chancellor succeeded in impressing the Soviets in a way in which a schooled diplomatist like Eden would never have been able to impress them. The gentlemen of the Kremlin had expected a crafty satellite-princeling. . . . Instead, they found a man who was in no wise inferior to them in obstinacy and who at the same time put his cards openly on the table and was never afraid to speak his mind to them.[15]

Even before the end of Adenauer's career, comparisons were being made between his statecraft and that of Bismarck—and not always, at least in the pages of the *Rheinischer Merkur,* to Bismarck's advantage[16]—and they have multiplied since his retirement. Despite Rudolf Augstein's scornful remark that one needs "a shot of panegy-

[13] *Ibid.,* p. 669.
[14] See Rodens, *Adenauer,* pp. 49 f.
[15] *Der Spiegel,* 21 September 1955, p. 10.
[16] See, for instance, Otto B. Roegele, "Christ und Staatsmann. Zum 80. Geburtstag Konrad Adenauers," *Rheinischer Merkur* (Köln), 6 January 1956, p. 3. Winston Churchill's remark in the House of Commons, which was widely quoted in Germany, did not go far enough for some of the Chancellor's followers. Churchill said that Adenauer was "the greatest German *since* Bismarck."

ric drunkenness" in order to think of the two statesmen together,[17] there are some obvious similarities. Like Bismarck, Adenauer believed that Germany's destiny depended upon the success of her foreign policy, and that domestic political considerations had to be subordinated to that. He also shared some of his great predecessor's prejudices (his abiding distrust of Russia, for example), as well as such ingredients of his style as his preference for fact rather than theory, his aversion to useless gestures (formal protests, for instance, which could not be expected to produce results) and his confidence in his own decisions.[18] On a more basic level, it may be suggested also that Adenauer brought to the conduct of Germany's foreign relations the same kind of passion and responsibility and proportion that characterized Bismarck's diplomacy.[19]

These qualities were also rooted in his past. In 1917, when he was elected Chief Mayor of Cologne, he spoke words that may be taken to describe the zeal with which he took up the far more difficult tasks of foreign policy thirty-two years later. "There is nothing better life can offer," he said, "than to allow a man to expend himself fully with all the strength of his mind and soul, and to devote his entire being to creative activity."[20] Throughout Adenauer's long career, this creative urge was directed and balanced by the juristic rationalism in which he was trained as a young man,[21] and by his religious faith; for these together deepened his sense of duty, gave him the kind of self-assurance possessed by the greatest of his predecessors, and contributed to what one of his admirers has delicately described as "a realism . . . which does not permit of any schism between moral

---

[17] Konrad Adenauer und seine Epoche" in *Die Ära Adenauer*, p. 59. He has also been compared to Adolphe Thiers and, recently, by Werner Richter, to George Washington.

[18] Werner Richter, "Voilà un homme," *ibid.*, p. 123.

[19] In his provocative work, *Adenauer und das neue Deutschland* (Recklinghausen, 1956), p. 115, Edgar Alexander uses the same passage from Max Weber that I have used above in discussing Bismarck. He does not refer to Bismarck in this connection, and, since he speaks elsewhere of Bismarck's "religious-moral indifferentism" (p. 111), would probably not think of doing so.

[20] Weymar, *Adenauer*, p. 61.

[21] *Deutsche Rundschau*, January 1956, p. 27.

principles and expediency in the sphere of political action."[22] It would be difficult to define the moral component of Adenauer's statecraft,[23] but its role was certainly more important in motivating him than considerations of personal power and prestige. He intimated as much himself when he said, on one occasion, that he hoped that, when his Chancellorship could be seen in perspective, it would be recognized that he had done his duty.

It may be noted in passing that, in contrast to Bismarck's expressions of his religious faith, which were often both eloquent and moving, Adenauer's utterances on the same subject were down to earth and almost matter of fact. In October 1950, when Dr. Gustav Heinemann resigned his post as Minister of the Interior because he opposed German participation in a European Army, Adenauer said:

> Heinemann takes the view that, since God has twice dashed the weapons from the hands of the Germans, they must not take them up for a third time. He feels that we must have patience and recognize the will of God in his earthly rule. Now, I don't want to go into the matter of religious devotion and faith in God as such. But when Herr Heinemann implored me to do nothing, I told him that in my view God had given us a head to think with, and arms and hands to act with.[24]

Together with the positive qualities mentioned here, Adenauer possessed traits that often militated against the success of his policies, if only by arousing the hostility of people with whom he had to work. His contempt for the great majority of mankind, which he once expressed by saying that it was a pity that God had limited human percipience but had placed no bounds on human stupidity,[25] was never well concealed; and it and his occasional lack of gratitude toward people who served him well added to the ranks of his opponents. His proneness to authoritarian behavior, which was the

[22] Alexander, *Adenauer,* p. 108.

[23] See Fritz René Allemann, *Bonn ist nicht Weimar* (Köln, 1956), p. 333.

[24] Weymar, *Adenauer,* p. 549; Rodens, *Adenauer,* p. 63; Alexander, *passim.* Dr. Heinemann, in January 1958, participated in the attack on Adenauer's policy discussed in section III below. See *Frankfurter Allgemeine Zeitung,* 24 January 1958, p. 1, and *Der Spiegel,* 5 January 1958, pp. 13-22.

[25] Rodens, *Adenauer,* pp. 42 f., 73; Golo Mann, "Der Staatsmann und sein Werk," in *Die Ära Adenauer,* p. 175.

subject of so many anecdotes, grew with the years and worried even his admirers.[26] It is probably not true that a spokesman for a Bundestag delegation once said to him, "Herr Bundeskanzler, we have not come here just to say '*Amen*' and '*Ja*' to everything you propose," and received the answer, "Gentlemen, '*Amen*' is not necessary—'*Ja*' will do fine";[27] but there is no doubt that many persons, including his coalition partners,[28] were alienated by his peremptory manner, his apparent belief that his decisions should be accepted without further cavil, and his growing tendency—which reached its most deplorable form in the debate on the *Spiegel* affair on 7 November 1962[29] to attribute the worst possible motives to his critics and opponents. These weaknesses were bad enough in the domestic sphere; in the international they were even more dangerous. Some of the Chancellor's gratuitous affronts to the Russians, for example, betrayed an almost foolhardy failure to understand, or at least to make allowances for, the psychology of a proud and powerful people.

Fully as serious was the Chancellor's inclination to keep foreign affairs to himself, a practice of which the Bundestag became increasingly critical. It is true that on occasion he permitted the Bundestag's Foreign Affairs Committee to play a part in his diplomacy—taking its members with him to Paris in 1954, for example, and to Moscow

[26] Alfred Grosser has expressed his concern by writing: "Under the weight of his personality, the Chancellor very extensively stifled the free play of democracy, the establishing and strengthening of which was so largely his own achievement." *Die Bonner Demokratie* (Düsseldorf, 1960), pp. 419 ff.

[27] Emmett J. Hughes in *Life*, 10 May 1954, p. 178.

[28] At the time of the coalition troubles of November 1955, *Der Spiegel* reprinted a cartoon from a Hamburg newspaper showing Adenauer, garbed as Frederick the Great, bringing a little dog to heel, with the words, "Dehler, komm' Er mal her!" Dehler was the leader of the dissident Free Democrats. *Der Spiegel*, 30 November 1955, p. 13.

[29] On this occasion the Chancellor caused a storm by accusing the editor of *Der Spiegel* of "systematically practising treason in order to make money," although the investigation of the magazine's activities, then under way, had not been completed and no formal charges had been filed. The incident heightened his own party's pressure for Adenauer's retirement, and it is still remembered to his discredit. See Rodens, *Adenauer*, pp. 35 ff.; Sidney Gruson in *New York Times*, 7 December 1962; and Paul Sethe in *Die Zeit*, 5 June 1964.

in 1955—but there was some feeling that he did this only when he wished to share responsibility for a failure.[30] Members of parliament were consequently less impressed by the rare examples of cooperation than they were by the great areas of foreign affairs from which they were excluded.

The *Deutsche Zeitung* once published a cartoon showing a gallant Adenauer in full evening dress kissing the hand of a beautiful gowned and exotically foreign woman, before going off to a rather dowdy and obviously Germanic one. He was saying, "I will be right back, my dearest. I've just got a duty dance to get over with."[31] Many deputies recognized themselves in that second feminine figure and were exasperated by the memory that, in the course of many dances of duty in the Bundestag, Adenauer had told them as little as possible about his affair with diplomacy. In parliamentary debate, the Chancellor was a master of the bland evasion, relying on remarks like the one made during the Saar debate of April 1954: "You will understand that, in the middle of negotiations, I can express myself only with great reserve about certain aspects of the . . . problem."[32] This sort of thing would have been easier to accept if it had not been for the suspicion that the reserve was not always justified. It was remembered, for example, that Adenauer offered German divisions to the Allied High Commission in a memorandum of 29 August 1950 and informed the Bundestag of this only eighteen months later, and then almost by chance.[33]

Even in the Foreign Ministry men who were supposed to be the Chancellor's official advisers often had the feeling of being uninformed and unwanted; and in the early days, when Adenauer served as both Chancellor and Foreign Minister, it was said that desk officers in the Ministry learned what was going on only by

---

[30] S. Wahrhaftig in *West German Leadership and Foreign Policy*, edited by Hans Speier and W. Phillips Davison (Evanston, 1957), p. 30.

[31] *Deutsche Zeitung und Wirtschaftszeitung*, 29 January 1955, p. 2.

[32] *Der Spiegel*, 5 May 1954, p. 5. See also *ibid.*, 26 March 1958, p. 13.

[33] Claus Jacobi, "Germany's Great Old Man," *Foreign Affairs*, xxxiii (January, 1955), 246. Adenauer did not invite the attention even of members of his own party to foreign policy. A cartoon in the *Westdeutsche Allgemeine Zeitung* showed a group of CDU members being kept after school to copy one hundred times the sentence: "The Federal Chancellor *alone* determines foreign policy." *Der Spiegel*, 26 March 1958, p. 3.

reading the *Neue Züricher Zeitung*. This situation was improved somewhat when Dr, Heinrich Brentano became Foreign Minister in 1955, although the coordination between the Chancellor and Brentano was not perfect; but when Gerhard Schröder took over the Foreign Ministry in 1962 the Chancellor tended to go his own way again, and there were instances in which he so clearly repudiated statements made by his Foreign Minister that confusion and irritation were aroused in the capitals of the Republic's allies. The Chancellor's preference for making policy by himself, which he shared with Bismarck, had some unfortunate results, and it has been said that the reason that he was surprised by the rude reception he received in Moscow in 1955 was that he relied more on his own guesses about what the Russians would be like than on expert advice.[34]

Adenauer's self-sufficiency was also to be noted in his attitude toward the diplomatic service. When a Bundestag committee asked him in 1954 why more comprehensive instructions and requests for information were not sent to representatives abroad, he is reported to have said, "Then they would talk too much!"[35] and he seems, indeed, to have wanted his diplomats to talk as little as possible either to him, in the form of reports, or to the governments to which they were accredited. Talleyrand's advice to young diplomats, *"Pas trop de zèle!"* he believed should be binding even on ambassadors in major posts, and he could be ruthless when it was flouted, as it was by his ambassador in Moscow early in 1962.[36] There was, on the other hand, at least one occasion on which he failed to support an envoy who had incurred the wrath of a foreign government through

---

[34] Wahrhaftig in *West German Leadership*, p. 34, is inclined to believe that there is a dearth of Russian specialists in Western Germany and this was the source of the trouble on the Moscow trip. Cf. H. von Borch, "Glossen," *Aussenpolitik*, vi (1955), 613 ff.

[35] *Der Spiegel*, 15 September 1954, p. 6.

[36] The differences between the ambassador, Dr. Hans Kroll, and the Foreign Office came to a head in March 1962, when it was reported that Kroll had recommended making major concessions to the Russians for a Berlin-German settlement. It seems clear that Kroll had exceeded his instructions, but the Chancellor's reaction, which led him among other things to publish the angry telegram recalling the ambassador, struck many as being unusually violent. See *New York Times*, 4 March 1962.

no fault of his own but because of abrupt changes of direction in Bonn.[37] All in all, Konrad Adenauer's behavior toward the members of his foreign service seems to have been as harmful to efficiency and morale as that of Bismarck.

The qualities that have been listed here, most of them fully developed long before Adenauer came to the chancellorship, were the components of his political style—a style that made him stand out conspicuously from the colorless ranks of the western statesmen of the postwar epoch. Anyone seeking to appraise his career as Chancellor will have to decide for himself how heavily to weigh his positive and negative traits as he analyzes the course and development of his foreign policy and the unsolved problems left in its wake.

II

When Konrad Adenauer became Chancellor of the new Federal Republic, which had resulted from the fusion of the three western occupation zones, he might theoretically have done what he is now reproached for not having done: he might have decided to devote all his energies to pursuing the idea of national unity and seeking the liberation of the seventeen million Germans in the Soviet zone. But, in 1949, the problem of reunification seemed less pressing than it did later, partly because recent Soviet actions made any accommodation seem impossible (the Berlin blockade was fresh in memory), partly because the questions that affected most citizens of the Federal Republic were bound up with the penalties still imposed on Western Germany by the Allies. It even seemed possible that any real attempt to press the reunification issue in 1949 might actually aggravate those problems, by annoying the British, by alarming the French, and even by reducing the Marshall aid upon which the German people were so dependent.[38]

[37] In May 1962, Ambassador W. Grewe in Washington was placed in an embarrassing position by the Chancellor's brusque repudiation of certain statements made by Foreign Minister Schröder to Secretary of State Dean Rusk and was subsequently subjected to such humiliating treatment in the White House that his position became untenable. The Chancellor made no attempt to come to his assistance. See Gerd Bucerius, "Adenauers Zeit is vorbei," in Die Zeit, 18 May 1962.
[38] Jacobi in Foreign Affairs, xxxiii, 240 f.

The risks Adenauer was not prepared to take. In his mind, the reunification issue occupied a position at least as remote as the problem of eastern frontiers did in Stresemann's, and probably more so; and like Stresemann Adenauer saw that the immediate problems were in the West. German recovery once more meant the removal of present burdens and disabilities, and the key to this, once more, was reconciliation with France. But the difference between Adenauer and Stresemann lay in the fact that Adenauer no longer thought of recovery as promising a return to an independent great-power position for his country. "When you fall from the heights as we Germans have done," he said on one occasion, "you realize that it is necessary to break with what has been. We cannot live fruitfully with false illusions."[39] The day of the Greater German Reich was over. This time reconciliation with the Allies and the regaining of German sovereignty must both serve the cause of western European unity.

Adenauer's policy has been called a blend of strategic realism and high-minded idealism.[40] Its realism was demonstrated in the action with which it was inaugurated, the conclusion of the Petersberg agreement in November 1949. This put an end to the dismantling process with respect to important sectors of German industry and, thus, performed incalculable good for the national economy. The price of the Allied concession was German adherence to the Ruhr Statute, which had been promulgated by the occupying powers in December 1948 and which had set up an international authority for the Ruhr. To nationalists, this was too high a price to pay. Adenauer, on the other hand, believed no price too high for the cessation of dismantling; and, since this was the one that was set, he thought it might as well be accepted cheerfully, in the hope that agreement here might create opportunities for the exaction of new concessions from the Allies. Parenthetically, it may be said that, as it turned out, Adenauer's calculation was correct; and his acceptance of the Ruhr Statute marked the beginning of the rapid disappearance of all limitations on German sovereignty.[41]

[39] Alexander, *Adenauer*, p. 17. Gösta von Uexküll, "Adenauer siegte bei Stalingrad," in *Die Ära Adenauer*, pp. 135 f.

[40] Henry Kellermann in *West German Leadership*, pp. 79 f.

[41] See F. R. Allemann, "Die Krise der deutschen Aussenpolitik," *Der Monat*, 8. Jahrg., Heft 89 (February, 1956), 5 f.

Yet, as has been indicated, there was more to this than realism. Since 1923 at least, Adenauer, the Rhinelander and Catholic, had thought of Germany as part of a western European community. In that year he had told the chairman of the Allied Rhineland Commission, M. Tirard, that "a lasting peace between France and Germany can only be attained through the establishment of a community of economic interests between the two countries,"[42] a community that would inevitably attract the other states of the West. This view had not changed.

In May 1949, in a speech at Berne, Adenauer indicated that he would support the Ruhr Statute, if it was "the beginning of a new order in the economy of all Western Europe . . . a promising starting point for general and comprehensive co-operation among the nations of Europe."[43] His formal acceptance of the statute in November marked the beginning of his fight to achieve this co-operation. This was the ideal that he held out to the German people, telling them over and over again that Germany could no longer be a great power by herself, that there were no longer *any* European great powers, and that the future lay in common European thought and action.[44]

We must free ourselves [he said in May 1953] from thinking in terms of national statehood. . . . West European countries are no longer in a position to protect themselves individually; none of them is any longer in a position to salvage European culture. These objectives . . . can only be attained if the West European nations form a political, economic and cultural union and, above all, if they render impossible any military conflicts among themselves.[45]

None of the other German statesmen considered in these lectures was capable of this kind of language. Not even Adenauer's

[42] See Fritz Stern, "Adenauer and a Crisis in Weimar Democracy," *Political Science Quarterly*, LXXIII (1958), 22 and note 55.

[43] Weymar, *Adenauer,* p. 389.

[44] For later expressions of this thought, see *Das Parlament* (Bonn), 29 January 1958, p. 14, and *Frankfurter Allgemeine Zeitung,* 30 January 1958, p. 5.

[45] Quoted by Kellermann in *West German Leadership,* p. 80. See also Konrad Adenauer, "Germany and Europe," *Foreign Affairs,* XXXI (1953), 366; Konrad Adenauer, "Germany, the New Partner," *ibid.,* XXXIII (1955), 181.

great antagonist, Kurt Schumacher of the Social Democratic party, was able to rise above nationalism to this degree. This was something new in German statecraft.

In the years from 1949 to 1954 Adenauer held before the German people the vision of the new European order, which would be founded on the twin pillars of the Coal and Steel Plan and the European Defense Community and which would be upheld by the good will of common men in all countries. That this vision captured the imagination of the German people was surely attested by the magnitude of the Chancellor's electoral victory in September 1953.[46] That his devotion to it convinced the Allies of his reliability was shown by the progressive removal of the remaining controls in Western Germany, although this process was doubtless facilitated also by the eagerness with which Western military authorities awaited the raising of German troops.[47] That the spirit with which he followed the idea of European unity communicated itself to the Federal Republic's neighbors was demonstrated by the way in which Italy and the Benelux countries stood by the Chancellor as he waged his fight for EDC at Brussels in the first days of August 1954. But, in the end, all this proved useless. Later in the terrible month of August, as Adenauer was to describe it, the French Assembly defeated EDC and removed European union from the sphere of practical politics.

How embittered the Chancellor was by this defeat was revealed by that now famous conversation in Claridge's during the London Conference, which was overheard by a reporter of the Hamburg news weekly, *Der Spiegel.* Speaking to M. Bech of Luxembourg and M. Spaak of Belgium, Adenauer expressed the gravest concern over the defeat of the Defense Community, and he repeatedly came back to the idea that the French action would lead to a revival of nationalism and militarism in Germany that would in time represent a danger to the whole continent. "I am firmly convinced," he is reported to have said, "one hundred per cent convinced, that the national army to which M. Mendés-France is forcing us will be a

[46] F. R. Allemann, "Bonn ist nicht Weimar," *Der Monat,* 7. Jahrg., Heft 76 (January, 1955), 333 ff.
[47] The military question cannot be treated at length here. See, *inter alia,* Lewis J. Edinger, *West German Rearmament* (Documentary Research Division, Air University, Maxwell Field, Ala., 1955).

great danger for Germany and Europe. When I am no longer on hand," he added somberly, "I don't know what will become of Germany, unless we still manage to create Europe in time."[48]

This was probably exaggerated—in view of the riots that soon broke out in Germany against the necessity of rearming, it certainly seems so—but it was deeply felt. And this bitterness persisted in the months that followed, as the Federal Republic was, in default of EDC, made a full-fledged member of NATO and as, at long last, it regained full sovereignty. In other circumstances, these would have been generally regarded as diplomatic triumphs of the first order. A Swiss newspaperman pointed out that, when one remembered the state of Germany in 1949, it was almost impossible to believe what had been accomplished since then, and that no more remarkable feat of statecraft could be imagined than Adenauer's transformation of Western Germany "into a partner no longer dictated to but wooed—and all this by means of a consistently pro-Allied policy."[49] Yet to many Germans, these accomplishments seemed a kind of second best, compared with the goal they had been seeking, while others who looked at what the Chancellor had achieved saw the price they would have to pay rather than the gains they were making.

Thus, in the months that stretched between the London and Paris conferences and the final ratification of the Paris treaties by the Bundestag in February 1955, the Chancellor was assailed by perfervid supporters of European union who, in their disillusionment, swung into opposition;[50] by politicians who considered his acceptance of the Saar Statute just as unpatriotic as they had considered his acceptance of the Petersberg agreement six years before;[51] by all those

---

[48] Der Spiegel, 6 October 1954, pp. 5 f. This article created a stir and was widely commented on in the German and foreign press. Its veracity was never disputed by Adenauer. For the circumstances of the conversation, see ibid., 13 October 1954, p. 4. For other expressions of Adenauer's views in these weeks, see The Times (London), 4 September 1954, p. 6.

[49] Lorenz Stucki, "Adenauer in Nöten," Die Weltwoche (Zürich), 5 November 1954, p. 1.

[50] See, for instance, Paul Sethe, "Es gibt noch Vaterländer," Frankfurter Allgemeine Zeitung, 11 November 1954.

[51] Ibid., 27 October, 1 November 1954. For a fuller discussion of the Saar question, see Edgar Alexander, Adenauer and the New Germany (New York, 1957) (a different version of the book cited above), pp. 179-202.

who—now that admission into an arms community had become actual —were frightened by the military costs and risks necessarily assumed;[52] and, most bitterly, by those who now said, and continued to say, that, in his pursuit of his Western objectives, Konrad Adenauer was making the reunification of Germany impossible.

III

Criticism of the Chancellor's policy towards the Soviet Union had been mounting ever since the death of Stalin and had recently been given a decided impetus by a speech of Heinrich Bruening before the Rhine-Ruhr Club in Düsseldorf in June 1954. In this address the former Chancellor charged that Adenauer's policy was too dogmatic and too pro-Western and that it would make the recovery of the German lands under Soviet control impossible. Germany should imitate the policy of the 1920's, Bruening said, the period in which—protected by the Rapallo, Locarno, and Berlin treaties—she had mediated between East and West, while at the same time enjoying the now long absent benefits of the eastern trade. The trouble with the people in Bonn, he said, was that they did not seem to have read those treaties."[53]

This singularly disconnected discourse completely overlooked the transformation in power relationships that had taken place since 1922, gave a misleading impression of the position of the Weimar Republic after 1926, and was entirely devoid of practical suggestions.[54] It was nevertheless bound to create a stir in a country where the word *Rapallo* always elicits a sentimental reaction, and it did so. Bruening's argument was echoed by Karl Georg Pfleiderer, and

---

[52] See, for instance, Gordon A. Craig, "NATO and the New German Army," in *Military Policy and National Security,* edited by W. W. Kaufmann (Princeton, 1956), pp. 218 ff.

[53] Heinrich Bruening, "Die Vereinigten Staaten und Europa. Ein Vortrag im Rhein-Ruhr-Club, Düsseldorf" (Stuttgart, 1954); *New York Times,* 5 June 1954, p. 4; *Manchester Guardian,* 7 June 1954, p. 5.

[54] For criticisms of Bruening's speech, see, *inter alia,* R.K., "Der Mythus von Rapallo," *Deutsche Zeitung,* 26 June 1954, p. 3; F. R. Allemann, "Zurück zu Rapallo?" *Der Monat,* 7. Jahrg., Heft 73 (October 1954), 42 ff., 47; the German edition of Alexander, *Adenauer,* especially pp. 143 ff.; "Bruenings Tragik auf deutscher Bühne," *Rheinischer Merkur,* 11 June 1954, p. 3.

before long these two were joined by ex-Chancellor Luther[55] and—
after the defeat of EDC—by a host of other dignitaries. By October,
the volatile leader of the Free Democrats, Thomas Dehler, had
leaped into the dispute by suggesting that a new approach be
made to Moscow, and the Social Democrats were insisting that the
NATO tie should not be consummated until an earnest new attempt had been made to clarify the reunification question by negotiations with the Soviet Union.[56]

In responding to these criticisms Adenauer showed both his strong-
est and his weakest characteristics. In the Bundestag debate on the
London agreement in October 1954, he was masterly, sitting all day
silent on the government bench until the evening, when the pro-
ceedings were broadcast, and then intervening again and again in
the debate, with well-calculated fits of rage, dismissing the opposition's arguments as trivial or as yesterday's outworn *Realpolitik,* and
insisting that the German people must accept the freedom that the
West now offered them.[57] Here and in subsequent debates he carried
the house and the people with him. But it should be noted that this
achievement was flawed by his attribution to his opponents of motives
meaner than his own and by his practice of intimating—unfairly
but in many subtle ways—that they were all neutralists or pro-
Communists. Moreover, and this was more important, throughout
the campaign he indulged his old penchant for oversimplification,
by repeatedly arguing that a policy of strength, founded on German
rearmament and adhesion to NATO, would force the Russians, in
due course, to grant reunification.

This was a dangerous argument to advance, even for the sake of
winning acceptance of the London and Paris agreements, for it was
bound to arouse unreasonable expectations. Basically, the flaw in the
theory that strength would lead to successful negotiation was that it
presupposed a willingness to use that strength if the objectives of
negotiation were not attained. But the Russians knew perfectly well
that, however strong the West became, it would not launch a war to

[55] *New York Times,* 6 June 1954, p. 9.
[56] F. R. Allemann, "Kein Urlaub von der Aussenpolitik," *Der Monat,* 7.
Jahrg., Heft 75 (Dec. 1954).
[57] See the account in *Der Spiegel,* 13 October 1954, p. 5. In the debate of
17 December 1954, he was less effective, apparently because of overwork.
Ibid., 22 December 1954, pp. 5-8.

achieve German reunification; and this should have been realized in Bonn and Washington before quite so much was said about Western expectations. In retrospect, it is still amazing that, on the eve of the first Geneva conference of 1955, the leaders of the Western alliance seem to have convinced themselves, or perhaps to have been convinced by Adenauer, that the Soviets were awed by western might and were—for this and other, principally economic, reasons—on the point of caving in.

Nothing that happened on the summit gave any support to that overconfident belief. Nor did anything that happened in the months that followed. Indeed, in September 1955, when Adenauer made his famous trip to Moscow, his hosts seem to have taunted him about his reliance on the policy of strength;[58] and then, exerting a little force of their own, pressured him into granting diplomatic recognition of the Soviet Union despite the fact that it was the patron of the other Germany.[59] Later in the year, at the meeting of foreign ministers at Geneva, the Soviet diplomats dispelled a lot of accumulated illusions by making it clear that they alone could grant German reunification and that they had no intention of doing so, except on their own terms.

The failure of the excessively optimistic expectations of the years

[58] *Ibid.*, 14 September 1955, pp. 9-14, 21 September, pp. 6-14; Borch in *Aussenpolitik*, vi, 613 ff.; Alexander, *Adenauer*, German ed., pp. 167 ff., American ed., pp. 215-38.

[59] The Chancellor was anxious to free German war prisoners still held in Russia, and recognition was the price he paid. The price was high. Hermann Proebst has written: "The Soviets had succeeded in creating a situation in which the Soviet Union alone among the victorious powers could henceforth and with full legality maintain diplomatic relations with the two German governments. They thereby won an advantage, insofar as this possibility was still denied the Western governments, who had pledged themselves to the recognition of the *Bundesrepublik* as the only legal representative of the German people. Basically, therefore, the Soviets had, in one important sense, established their theory of two German states." "Zu früh und zu spät," in *Die Ära Adenauer*, p. 157. This perhaps goes too far, but it cannot be denied that the recognition violated the spirit of the Hallstein Doctrine, which denied recognition to all states maintaining formal relations with the so-called German Democratic Republic (DDR). See Rüdiger Altmann, "Leitbilder deutscher Aussenpolitik," in *Die Zeit*, 9 November 1962, or the chapter of the same name in his book *Das deutsche Risiko* (Stuttgart, 1962). Dr. Hallstein, who went to Moscow with Adenauer, pointed out the contradiction but was overborne.

1953-55 beclouded the second phase of Adenauer's direction of his country's foreign policy. The Suez and Hungarian crises of 1956 demonstrated the basic fallacy of the liberation policy preached so sedulously by his warmest friend among Western statesmen, John Foster Dulles, and also came close to destroying the NATO alliance. The launching of the Sputniks in 1957 indicated that the theory that the Soviets were getting weaker was, at least in the military sense, the reverse of the truth; and the Berlin note of Premier Khrushchev in November 1958 seemed to reflect a dangerous confidence on the part of the Soviet government.[60] Even if the fears originally aroused by that note were not borne out, the shock was enough to intensify criticism of the Adenauer line, and this criticism reached its height on 13 August 1961, when the Ulbricht government erected the Wall in Berlin without effective opposition from the Chancellor and his allies.

In the years during which Western strength seemed to be declining while Soviet might and intransigence mounted, the cry was frequently raised that Adenauer had failed to sound out the Russians at a time when an accommodation with them would have been possible. This argument was usually based upon accusations made by two of his former ministers to the effect that he had willfully refused, and had persuaded his allies to refuse, to give serious consideration to a Soviet note of 10 March 1952, which, they claimed, if properly followed up, might have led to the recovery at least of Middle Germany on acceptable terms, and probably with free elections.[61]

It is obvious that these are charges that are impossible, at this historical remove, to prove or disprove. Yet it may well be that this debate has revealed the question upon which any final assessment of Konrad Adenauer will turn. For, as one reads the Soviet note of March 1952, the salient point is not the one over which the

---

[60] See Rüdiger Altmann in *Die Zeit*, 9 November 1962.

[61] On the Soviet note in question, see *New York Times*, 11 March 1952, p. 1, and the editorial "A New Soviet Maneuver," *ibid.*, 12 March 1952, p. 26. On the debate of January 1958, see *ibid.*, 30 January 1958, p. 4; *Frankfurter Allgemeine Zeitung*, 30 January 1958; Erich Dombrowski, "Der vorbeigegangene Dolchstoss," *ibid.*, 31 January 1958; F. R. Allemann in *Die Zeit* (Hamburg), 31 January 1958; *Rheinischer Merkur*, 31 January 1958, pp. 1-2; and *Das Parlament*, 29 January 1958, esp. pp. 8, 19-22.

publicists were still arguing after his retirement[62]—namely, whether it was a sincere offer or merely an elaborate maneuver—but rather the fact that the Western powers and their German partner did not apparently make any serious effort to find out, by exploration and negotiation, how sincere it might be. And that, as Claus Jacobi wrote some years ago in another connection, "is why the Federal Republic in its reunification policy lacks the alibi which it probably could have had quite easily. And since history is resentful, it will—[we should perhaps say 'may']—one day ask where this alibi is."[63]

Adenauer's last years of office were not his happiest. The dignity that had always surrounded his figure was damaged by the curious episode in 1959, when he announced that he was willing to move from the Chancellorship to the post of *Bundespräsident* and then reversed himself when it was determined that his exaggerated views of the powers he would possess in his new position had no constitutional validity; and the *Spiegel* affair of 1962 threw such a cruel light upon the anti-democratic behavior of some of his ministerial colleagues that it seriously weakened confidence in his cabinet and, indeed, his personal leadership. These deplorable affairs and the Wall overshadowed his last diplomatic triumph—the fulfillment of his old ambition to complete the reconciliation of France and Germany. On the day of his induction as Federal Chancellor on 20 September 1949 Adenauer had told the Bundestag that "the Franco-German antagonism, which has dominated European politics for hundreds of years and given occasion for so many wars and so much destruction and bloodshed, must finally be unconditionally removed from the world."[64] He had made the first long step toward that goal when he negotiated the Saar Treaty of 27 October 1956;[65] and in July 1962 he crowned the great endeavor during the visit to Paris which led to the Franco-German treaty of the following January.[66] Yet even this success seemed flawed; and, after Charles de Gaulle

[62] See Marion Gräfin Dönhoff, *Die Bundesrepublik in der Ära Adenauer: Kritik und Perspektiven* (Hamburg, 1963), pp. 203 ff.

[63] Jacobi in *Foreign Affairs*, xxxiii, 241; Augstein in *Die Ära Adenauer*, p. 63.

[64] Rodens, *Adenauer*, p. 161.

[65] *Ibid.*, p. 128.

[66] *Frankfurter Allgemeine Zeitung*, 6 July 1962; *Die Welt*, 6 July 1962; *Berliner Tagesspiegel*, 8 July 1962; *New York Times*, 22 January 1963.

had vetoed Great Britain's entrance into the Common Market on 29 January 1963, one writer held that this proved that, in seeking reconciliation with France, the Chancellor had unwittingly undermined his own hopes of European unity. "For thirteen years," she wrote, "against every kind of opposition, he steered the Federal Republic, with great patience and persistence, into the Western camp and tied it there, without consideration for reunification, which many people think might have been won at the price of neutralization. He placed the western community above reunification and now is sacrificing this community for the sake of the friendship that binds him to General de Gaulle."[67]

Of this judgment, as of many others passed on Adenauer's work in the last years of his office, one can only say that time alone will determine whether or not it is justified. There is no reason yet to throw the baby out with the bathwater; and it is possible, contrary to the opinion just quoted, that the movement towards some form of European federation has already gone so far that General de Gaulle's actions can have at worst only a decelerating effect.[68] And surely, in any case, the Franco-German reconciliation is in itself important.[69] Apart from this, and with reference once more to the issue of reunification, it is difficult to find anything in the pattern of Soviet behavior during the Adenauer years to indicate that the Soviet Union would or could have tolerated a neutralized united Germany at any time.[70] That being so, a departure from the Western line in order to follow this particular will-o-the-wisp might have led into very dangerous country indeed. As one of Adenauer's sternest critics has written, it is possible that the much criticized lack of movement in Adenauer's policy in his last years prevented mistakes that might have been irretrievable.[71] If there was one precept of classical diplomacy that Adenauer always honored it was that failure to resolve a problem is less dangerous than solving it in the wrong way.

---

[67] Marion Gräfin Dönhoff, "Ein schwarzer Tag," in *Die Zeit,* 1 February 1963.

[68] See, for instance, Achille Albonetti, "The New Europe and the West" in the "A New Europe?" issue of *Daedalus* (Winter, 1964).

[69] See Alfred Grosser's remarks quoted in Rodens, *Adenauer,* p. 130.

[70] See Altmann in *Die Zeit,* 9 November 1962.

[71] Augstein in *Die Ära Adenauer,* p. 82.

IV

Some of the sour comment that accompanied the Chancellor's departure from office seemed to have been written either by people who had forgotten the problems that faced him when he entered it or by publicists who were too young to have appreciated them properly. Yet surely it was no mean diplomatic achievement to have led fifty-three million dazed, disoriented and universally detested people from the hopelessness in which the war left them to a condition of economic prosperity, internal political stability, and membership in an alliance system in which their country was once more respected and accepted as an equal.[72] If the turn of events shows in the end that this was not enough or that the road chosen was the wrong one, it may well be that history will attribute this to Konrad Adenauer's frailties of character or statecraft. But at least no one will be able to charge that his failure was due to moral or political irresponsibility or to chauvinism or to lust for conquest. Among all the statesmen considered here, he is the one most free from that corrosive nationalism that has in the past distorted the German spirit. The nation whose unity was first forged by Bismarck he wished to submerge in a greater unity. Even failure should not be allowed to dim the grandeur of the attempt.

[72] See Matthias Walden, "Keine Alternative" in *Die Ära Adenauer,* pp. 161 f.

BIBLIOGRAPHY OF WORKS CITED

"A New Europe?" Special Issue of *Daedalus*, Journal of the American Academy of Arts and Sciences (Winter, 1964).

d'Abernon, Edgar Viscount. *An Ambassador of Peace* (3 vols., London, 1929-30).

Adenauer, Konrad. "Germany and Europe," *Foreign Affairs*, XXXI (1953).

―― "Germany, the New Partner," *Foreign Affairs*, XXXIII (1955).

Aera Adenauer, Die. Edited by Janko Musuliñ (Frankfurt am Main, 1964).

Alexander, Edgar. *Adenauer und das neue Deutschland* (Recklinghausen, 1956).

――*Adenauer and the New Germany* (New York, 1957).

Allemann, F. R. "Bonn ist nicht Weimar," *Der Monat*, 7. Jahrg., Heft 75 (December, 1954).

――*Bonn ist nicht Weimar* (Köln, 1956).

――"Die Krise der deutschen Aussenpolitik," *Der Monat*, 8. Jahrg., Heft 89 (February, 1956).

――"Kein Urlaub von der Aussenpolitik," *Der Monat*, 7. Jahrg., Heft 75 (December, 1954).

――"Zurück zu Rapallo?", *Der Monat*, 7. Jahrg., Heft 73 (October, 1954).

Altmann, Rüdiger. *Das deutsche Risiko* (Stuttgart, 1962).

――"Leitbilder deutscher Aussenpolitik," *Die Zeit*, 9 November, 1962.

Andreas, Willy. "Kiderlen-Wächter: Randglossen zu seinem Nachlass," *Historische Zeitschrift*, CXXXXX (1925).

Auswärtige Politik Preussens: Diplomatische Aktenstücke (herausgegeben von der Historischen Reichskommission, Oldenburg, 1931 ff.).

Aydelotte, William O. "The First German Colony and its Diplomatic Consequences," *Cambridge Historical Journal*, V (1937).

Bennett, Edward W. *Germany and the Diplomacy of the Financial Crisis, 1931* (Cambridge, Mass., 1962).

Bergmann, Carl. *The History of Reparations* (London, 1927).

Bernhardi. *Aus dem Leben Theodor von Bernhardis* (8 vols., Leipzig, 1893-1906).

Bismarck, Otto von. *Bismarck Gespräche*, herausgegeben von Willy Andreas unter Mitwirkung von K. F. Reinking. III: Von der Entlassung bis zum Tode. (Bremen, 1963).

———*Fürst Bismarcks Briefe an seine Braut und Gattin*, herausgegeben von Fürst Herbert Bismarck (Stuttgart, 1900).

———*Die gesammelten Werke* (15 vols. in 19, Berlin, 1924 ff.).

Blücher, Wipert von. *Deutschlands Weg nach Rapallo* (Wiesbaden, 1951).

Bonn, M. J. *Wandering Scholar* (New York, 1948).

Borch, H. von. "Glossen," *Aussenpolitik*, VI (1955).

Borries, Kurt. *Preussen im Krimkrieg* (Stuttgart, 1930).

Bracher, K. D. *Die Auflösung der Weimarer Republik* (2. Aufl., Stuttgart, 1957).

Brandenburg, Erich. *From Bismarck to the First World War* (London, 1933).

Brauer, Arthur von. "Die deutsche Diplomatie unter Bismarck," *Deutsche Revue* XXXI (2), (1906).

———*Im Dienste Bismarcks: Persönliche Erinnerungen*, herausgegeben von Helmuth Rogge (Berlin, 1936).

Bretton, Henry L. *Stresemann and the Revision of Versailles* (Stanford, 1953).

Bruening, Heinrich. "Die Vereinigten Staaten und Europa. Ein Vortrag im Rhein-Ruhr-Club, Düsseldorf" (Stuttgart, 1954).

Bucerius, Gerd. "Adenauers Zeit ist vorbei," *Die Zeit*, 18 May 1962.

Büchmann, Georg. *Geflügelte Wörter* (Volksausgabe nach der 29. Aufl., Berlin, 1943).

Bülow, Bernhard Fürst von. *Denkwürdigkeiten* (4 vols., Berlin, 1930-31).

Bullock, Alan. *Hitler: A Study in Tyranny* (Rev. ed., New York, 1962, Harper Torchbook edition, 1964).

Busch, Moritz. *Tagebuchblätter* (2 vols., Leipzig, 1899).

Clay, Lucius D. *Decision in Germany* (New York, 1950).

Craig, Gordon A. "Bismarck and his Ambassadors: The Problem of Discipline," *Foreign Service Journal*, XXXIII (June, 1956).

———"Great Britain and the Belgian Railways Dispute," *American Historical Review*, L (1945), 738-761.

———"Military Diplomats in the Prussian and German Service: The Attachés, 1816-1914," *Political Science Quarterly*, LXIV, (1949).

——"NATO and the New German Army" in *Military Policy and National Security*, edited by W. W. Kaufmann (Princeton, 1956).

——*The Politics of the Prussian Army, 1640-1945* (Oxford, 1955).

Curtius, Julius. *Sechs Jahre Minister der deutschen Republik* (Heidelberg, 1948).

Degras, Jane. *Soviet Documents on Foreign Policy*, I (Oxford, 1951).

The Diplomats, 1919-1939, edited by Gordon A. Craig and Felix Gilbert (Princeton, 1953).

Dirksen, Herbert von. *Moskau, Tokio, London: Erinnerungen und Betrachtungen zu 20 Jahren Aussenpolitik, 1919-39* (Stuttgart, 1950).

——*Moscow, Tokyo, London: Twenty Years of German Foreign Policy* (Norman, Okla., 1952).

I Documenti Diplomatici Italiani, edited by the Ministry of Foreign Affairs (Rome, 1952 ff.).

Documents Diplomatiques Français, edited by the French Foreign Ministry.

Documents on British Foreign Policy, 1919-1939, edited by E. L. Woodward and Rohan Butler (London, 1946 ff.).

Documents on German Foreign Policy, 1918-1945 (Washington, 1949 ff.).

Döblin, Alfred. "Republik," *Die neue Rundschau* (1920/1).

Dönhoff, Marion Gräfin. *Die Bundesrepublik in der Ära Adenauer: Kritik und Perspektiven* (Hamburg, 1963).

——"Ein schwarzer Tag," *Die Zeit*, 1 February 1963.

Dombrowski, E. "Der vorbeigegangene Dolchstoss," *Frankfurter Allgemeine Zeitung*, 31 January 1958.

Duncker, Max. *Politische Briefwechsel aus seinem Nachlass*, herausgegeben von J. Schultze (Stuttgart, 1923).

Edinger, Lewis J. *West German Rearmament* (Maxwell Field, Ala., 1955).

Edwards, Marvin L. *Stresemann and the Greater Germany, 1914-1918* (New York, 1962).

Einem, Generaloberst von. *Erinnerungen eines Soldaten, 1853-1933* (Leipzig, 1933).

Erdmann, K. D. "Das Problem der Ost— oder Westorientierung in der Locarno Politik Stresemanns," *Geschichte in Wissenschaft und Unterricht*, VI (1955).

Eschenburg, Theodor. *Die improvisierte Demokratie: Gesammelte Aufsätze zur Weimarer Republik* (München, 1963).

———*Das Kaiserreich am Scheideweg: Bassermann, Bülow und der Block* (Berlin, 1925).

Eyck, Erich. *Bismarck: Leben und Werk* (3 vols., Zürich, 1941-44).

———*Geschichte der Weimarer Republik* (2 vols., Zürich, 1954-56).

———"Neues Licht auf Stresemanns Politik," *Deutsche Rundschau*, 81. Jahrg. (1955).

Falckenstein, Trütschler von. "Kontroversen über die Politik Bismarcks in Jahre 1887," *Archiv für Politik und Geschichte*, VI (1926).

Fest, J. C. *Das Gesicht des Dritten Reiches: Profile einer totalitären Herrschaft* (München, 1963).

Fischer, Fritz. *Griff nach der Weltmacht* (Düsseldorf, 1962).

Fischer, Louis. *The Soviets in World Affairs* (new edition, 2 vols., Princeton, 1951).

Fontane, Theodor. *Briefe an Friedländer* (Berlin, 1954).

———*Briefe an seine Freunde* (2 vols., Berlin, 1925).

Foreign Relations of the United States, edited by the Department of State, Washington, D. C.

François-Poncet, André. *Souvenirs d'une ambassade à Berlin* (Paris, 1946).

Frank, Walther. "Der geheime Rat Paul Kayser," *Historische Zeitschrift*, CLXVIII (1943).

Freund, Gerald. *Unholy Alliance* (New York, 1957).

Freytag, Gustav. "Freytags Briefe an Stosch," *Deutsche Revue*, XXXVII (3), (1912).

Freytag-Loringhoven, Freiherr von. *Menschen und Dinge wie ich sie in meinem Leben sah* (Berlin, 1923).

Front wider Bülow, herausgegeben von F. Thimme (München, 1931).

Gasiorowski, Zygmunt J. "Stresemann and Poland before Locarno," *Journal of Central European Affairs*, XVIII (1958).

Gatzke, Hans W. *Germany's Drive to the West: A Study of Germany's Western War Aims during the First World War* (Baltimore, 1950).

———"Gustav Stresemann: A Bibliographical Article," *Journal of Modern History*, XXXVI (1964).

———"Russo-German Military Collaboration during the Weimar Republic," *American Historical Review*, LXIII (1958).

———*Stresemann and the Rearmament of Germany* (Baltimore, 1954).

———"Von Rapallo nach Berlin: Stresemann und die deutsche Russlandpolitik," *Vierteljahrshefte für Zeitgeschichte*, IV (1956).

Gessler, Otto. *Reichswehrpolitik in der Weimarer Zeit,* herausgegeben von Kurt Sendtner (Stuttgart, 1958).

Geyl, Jürgen. *Austria, Germany and the Anschluss, 1931-38* (New York, 1963).

Geyr von Schweppenburg, Freiherr. *Erinnerungen eines Militär-attachés: London, 1933-37* (Stuttgart, 1949).

Giannini, Amedeo. *Saggi di storia diplomatica, 1920-40* (Firenze, 1940).

Gisevius, Hans Bernd. *Adolf Hitler: Versuch einer Deutung* (München, 1963).

Göhring, Martin. *Stresemann, Mensch, Staatsmann, Europäer: Gedenkrede, gehalten am 8. Juli 1956* (Mainz, 1956).

Görlitz, Walter. *Gustav Stresemann* (Heidelberg, 1947).

Goldschmidt, Hans. "Mitarbeiter Bismarcks im aussenpolitischen Kampf," *Preussische Jahrbücher,* CCXXXVI (1934).

Gooch, G. P. *Studies in Diplomacy* (London, 1942).

Groener, Wilhelm. *Lebenserinnerungen,* herausgegeben von F. Freiherr Hiller von Gärtringen (Göttingen, 1957).

Die Grosse Politik der Europäischen Kabinette, 1871-1914: Sammlung der diplomatischen Akten des Auswärtigen Amtes (Berlin, 1921 ff.).

Grosser, Alfred. *Die Bonner Demokratie* (Düsseldorf, 1960).

Hagen, M. von. *Bismarck und England* (Stuttgart, 1941).

Haller, Fritz. *Philipp Eulenburg, the Kaiser's Friend* (2 vols., London, 1930).

Hallgarten, George W. F. "Fritz von Holsteins Geheimnis," *Historische Zeitschrift,* CLXXVII (1954).

———"General Hans von Seeckt and Russia, 1920-22," *Journal of Modern History,* XXI (1949).

Hammann, Otto. *Bilder aus der letzten Kaiserzeit* (Berlin, 1922).

d'Harcourt, Robert Comte. *Konrad Adenauer* (Paris, 1955).

Hartung, Fritz. "Bismarck und Arnim," *Historische Zeitschrift,* CLXXI (1951).

———"Verantwortliche Regierung, Kabinette und Nebenregierungen im konstitutionellen Preussen 1848-1914," *Forschungen zur brandenburgischen und preussischen Geschichte,* XLIV (1932).

Hatzfeldt, Paul von. "Bismarck und Napoleon III. Erinnerungen des Botschafters Hatzfeldt," *Berliner Monatshefte,* 18. Jahrg. (1940).

Hauser, Oswald, "Der Plan einer Deutsch-Oesterreichischen Zollunion von 1931 und die europäische Föderation," *Historische Zeitschrift,* CLXXIX (1955).

Helbig, Herbert. "Die Moskauer Mission des Grafen Brockdorff-Rant-
zau," *Forschungen zur Osteuropäischen Geschichte*, II (1955).
———*Die Träger der Rapallo Politik* (Göttingen, 1958).
Hiller von Gärtringen, F. Freiherr. *Fürst Bülows Denkwürdigkeiten:
Untersuchungen zu ihrer Entstehungsgeschichte und ihrer Kritik*
(Tübingen, 1956).
Hitler, Adolf. *Hitler Directs His War: The Secret Records of His Daily
Military Conferences*, edited by Felix Gilbert (New York, 1950).
———*The Speeches of Adolf Hitler*, edited by Norman H. Baynes (Ox-
ford, 1942).
———*Hitler's Secret Conversations*, edited by H. R. Trevor-Roper (New
York, 1953).
Hohenlohe-Schillingsfürst, Prinz Chlodwig zu. *Denkwürdigkeiten der
Reichskanzlerzeit*, herausgegeben von K. A. von Müller (Stutt-
gart, 1931).
Holborn, Hajo. "Bismarck und Werthern," *Archiv für Politik und Ges-
chichte*, V (1925-26).
Holl, Karl. *Gesammelte Aufsätze zur Kirchengeschichte: I. Luther* (6.
Aufl., Tübingen, 1932).
The Holstein Papers, edited by Norman Rich and M. H. Fisher (4 vols.,
Cambridge, 1955 ff.).
Hoover, Herbert. *The Memoirs of Herbert Hoover: III. The Great
Depression, 1929-41* (New York, 1952).
Horkenbach, Cuno. *Das deutsche Reich von 1918 bis heute* (Berlin,
1930).
House, Edward. *The Intimate Papers of Colonel House* (4 vols., Bos-
ton, 1926 ff.).
Hubatsch, W. "Die deutsche Berufsdiplomatie im Kriege," *Aussen-
politik*, VI (1955).
Hutten-Czapski, Bogdan Graf. *Sechzig Jahre Politik und Gesellschaft* (2
vols., Berlin, 1935-36).

Jacobi, Claus. "Germany's Great Old Man," *Foreign Affairs*, XXXIII
(1955).
Jäckh, Ernst. *Kiderlen-Wächter: Der Staatsmann und der Mensch* (2
vols., Berlin and Leipzig, 1925).

Kardorff, S. von. *Wilhelm von Kardorff* (Berlin, 1936).
Kerr, Alfred. *Caprichos: Strophen des Nebenstroms* (Berlin, 1926).
Kessler, Harry Graf. *Tagebücher* (Frankfurt am Main, 1962).
———*Walther Rathenau: His Life and Work* (New York, 1930).

Kohn, Hans, ed. *German History: Some New German Views* (Boston, 1954).

Kollmann, Eric. "Walther Rathenau and German Foreign Policy: Thoughts and Actions," *Journal of Modern History,* XXIV (1952).

Kordt, Erich. *Nicht aus den Akten* (Stuttgart, 1950).

Krausnick, H. "Botschafter Graf Hatzfeldt und die Aussenpolitik Bismarcks," *Historische Zeitschrift,* CLXVII (1943).

———*Holsteins Geheimpolitik in der Ära Bismarck, 1886-90* (2. Aufl., Hamburg, 1942).

Kühlmann, Richard von. *Erinnerungen* (Heidelberg, 1948).

Lambsdorff, Gustav Graf von. *Die Militärbevollmächtigten Kaiser Wilhelms II. am Zarenhofe, 1904-1914* (Berlin, 1937).

Lancken Wackenitz, Oscar Freiherr von der. *Meine dreissig Dienstjahre* (Berlin, 1931).

Langer, W. L. *European Alliances and Alignments* (2nd ed., New York, 1950).

Lockhart, R. Bruce. *Retreat from Glory* (New York, 1934).

Mann, Thomas. *Doktor Faustus: Das Leben des deutschen Tonsetzers Adrian Leverkühn, erzählt von einem Freunde* (Stockholm, 1947).

Marcks, Erich. *Otto von Bismarck: Ein Lebensbild* (Stuttgart, 1915).

Meinck, Gerhard. *Hitler und die deutsche Aufrüstung, 1933-37* (Wiesbaden, 1959).

Meinecke, Friedrich. "Bismarcks Eintritt in den christlich-germanischen Kreis," *Historische Zeitschrift,* XC (1903).

Mendelssohn-Bartholdy, A. *The War and German Society* (New Haven, 1937).

Meyer, A. O. *Bismarck, der Mensch und der Staatsmann* (Stuttgart, 1949).

———*Bismarcks Glaube* (4. Aufl., München, 1933).

———*Bismarcks Kampf mit Oesterreich am Bundestag zu Frankfurt* (Berlin and Leipzig, 1927).

Meyer, Henry Cord. *Mitteleuropa in German Thought and Action* (The Hague, 1955).

Michael, Horst. *Bismarck, England und Europa* (München, 1930).

Mills, J. Saxon. *The Genoa Conference* (New York, 1922).

Monts, A. Graf von. *Erinnerungen und Gedanken,* herausgegeben von K. Nowak and F. Thimme (Berlin, 1932).

Muralt, Leonhard von. *Bismarcks Verantwortlichkeit* (Göttingen, 1955).
Muschg, Walter. "Deutschland ist Hamlet," *Die Zeit*, 1 May 1964.

Nadolny, Rudolf. *Mein Beitrag* (Wiesbaden, 1955).
Neubacher, Hermann. *Sonderauftrag Südost, 1940-45* (2. Aufl., Göttingen, 1957).
Nicolson, Harold. *Curzon: The Last Phase, 1919-25* (new ed., New York, 1939).

Olden, Rudolf. *Stresemann* (Berlin, 1929).

Pahlmann, Franz. "Der Stand des Gesprächs über Bismarcks Glauben," *Geschichte in Wissenschaft und Unterricht*, VII (1956).
Petrie, Sir Charles. *Life and Letters of the Right Honourable Sir Austen Chamberlain* (2 vols., London, 1939-40).
Pflanze, Otto. *Bismarck and the Development of Germany: The Period of Unification, 1815-1871* (Princeton, 1963).
Picker, Henry. *Hitlers Tischgespräche im Führerhauptquartier 1941-42,* neu herausgegeben von Percy Ernst Schramm (Stuttgart, 1963).

Radowitz, J. M. von. *Aufzeichnungen und Erinnerungen,* herausgegeben von Hajo Holborn (2 vols., Stuttgart, 1925).
Rahn, Rudolf. *Ruheloses Leben* (Düsseldorf, 1949).
Raschdau, Ludwig. *Unter Bismarck und Caprivi* (2. Aufl., Berlin, 1939).
———*Wie ich Diplomat wurde* (Berlin, 1938).
Rassow, Peter. "Schlieffen und Holstein," *Historische Zeitschrift*, CLXXIII (1952).
Rathenau, Walther. *Gesammelte Reden* (Berlin, 1924).
———*Walther Rathenau: Ein preussischer Europäer: Briefe,* herausgegeben von Margarete von Eynern (Berlin, 1955).
Raumer, Hans von. "Dreissig Jahre nach Rapallo," *Deutsche Rundschau*, 78. Jahrg., (1952).
———"Walther Rathenau," *Deutsche Rundschau*, 78. Jahrg. (1952).
Rauschning, Hermann. *Gespräche mit Hitler* (Zürich, 1940).
"Records of Modern Germany," *Times* [London] *Literary Supplement*, 10 June 1955.
Rein, Gustav Adolf. *Die Revolution in der Politik Bismarcks* (Göttingen, 1957).
Reiners, Ludwig. *Bismarck* (2 vols., München, 1956-57).

———*Stilkunst: Ein Lehrbuch deutscher Prosa* (4. Aufl., München, 1951).

Remak, Joachim. "Hitlers Amerikapolitik," *Aussenpolitik*, VI (1955).

Rheinbaben, W. Freiherr von. "Deutsche Ostpolitik in Locarno," *Aussenpolitik*, IV (1953).

Rich, Norman. "Holstein and the Arnim Affair," *Journal of Modern History*, XXVIII (1956).

Ritter, Gerhard. *Der Schlieffenplan: Kritik eines Mythos* (München, 1956).

Rodens, Franz. *Konrad Adenauer: Der Mensch und Politiker* (München, 1963).

Roegele, Otto B. "Christ und Staatsmann. Zum 80. Geburtstag Konrad Adenauers," *Rheinischer Merkur*, 6 January 1956.

Rogge, Helmuth. *Holstein und Hohenlohe: Neue Beiträge zu Friedrich von Holsteins Tätigkeit als Mitarbeiter Bismarcks und als Tatgeber Hohenlohes, 1874-1894* (Stuttgart, 1957).

Roon, Albrecht Graf von. *Denkwürdigkeiten* (5. Aufl., 3 vols., Berlin, 1905).

Rothfels, Hans. "Die Erinnerungen des Botschafters Radowitz," *Archiv für Politik und Geschichte*, IV (1925).

———"Sinn und Grenzen des Primats der Aussenpolitik," *Aussenpolitik*, VI (1955).

Rothfritz, Herbert. *Die Politik des preussischen Botschafters Grafen Robert von der Goltz* (Berlin, 1934).

Seabury, Paul. *The Wilhelmstrasse* (New York, 1955).

Scheele, Godfrey. *The Weimar Republic* (London, 1946).

Schieder, Theodor. "Die Probleme des Rapallo-Vertrags," *Arbeitsgemeinschaft für Forschung des Landes Nordrhein-Westfalen: Geisteswissenschaften*, Heft 43 (Köln, 1956).

Schlieffen, Generalfeldmarschall Graf Alfred. *Briefe*, herausgegeben von Eberhard Kessel (Göttingen, 1958).

Schlözer, Kurd von. *Petersburger Briefe*, herausgegeben von Leopold von Schlözer (Stuttgart, 1921).

———*Letzte römische Briefe*, herausgegeben von Leopold von Schlözer (Stuttgart, 1924).

Schmidt, Paul. *Statist auf diplomatischer Bühne, 1923-45* (Bonn, 1949).

Schüssler, Wilhelm. *Die Daily-Telegraph-Affaire: Fürst Bülow, Kaiser Wilhelm und die Krise des zweiten Reiches 1908* (Göttingen, 1952).

———*Um das Geschichtsbild* (Gladbeck, 1953).

Schütz, W. W. "Politik als Kunst des Notwendigen," *Aussenpolitik*, VII (1956).

Schulthess' Europäischer Geschichtskalender 1930 (München, 1931).

Schweinitz, H. L. von. *Denkwürdigkeiten*, herausgegeben von W. von Schweinitz (2 vols., Berlin, 1927).

Sethe, Paul. "Gibt es noch Vaterländer?" *Frankfurter Allgemeine Zeitung*, 11 November 1954.

Sontag, R. J. *Germany and England: Background of Conflict* (New York, 1938).

Spitzemberg. *Das Tagebuch der Baronin Spitzemberg: Aufzeichnungen aus der Hofgesellschaft des Hohenzollernreiches*, herausgegeben von Rudolf Vierhaus (Göttingen, 1960).

Srbik, H. Ritter von. *Deutsche Einheit* (4 vols., München, 1935-42).

Stambrook, F. G. "The German-Austrian Customs Union Project of 1931: A Study of German Methods and Motives," *Journal of Central European Affairs*, XXI (1961).

Stern, Fritz. "Adenauer and a Crisis in Weimar Democracy," *Political Science Quarterly*, LXXIII (1958).

Stössinger, Felix. "Die Wahrheit über Rapallo," *Deutsche Rundschau*, 78. Jahrg. (1952).

Stosch, Albrecht von. *Denkwürdigkeiten*, herausgegeben von Ulrich von Stosch (Stuttgart, 1904).

Stresemann, Gustav. *Vermächtnis*, herausgegeben von H. Bernhard (3 vols., Berlin, 1932-33).

Stucki, Lorenz. "Adenauer in Nöten," *Die Weltwoche*, 5 November 1954.

Studnitz, H. G. von. "Gesandte und Geschickte," *Der Monat*, 10. Jahrg., Heft 112 (1958).

———"Gestalt und Aufbau des Auswärtigen Amtes," *Aussenpolitik*, III (1952).

Swinton, Viscount. *I Remember* (London, 1946).

Sylvester, A. J. *The Real Lloyd George* (London, 1947).

Thimme, Anneliese, *Gustav Stresemann: Eine politische Biographie zur Geschichte der Weimarer Republik* (Hannover, 1957).

———"Gustav Stresemann, Legende und Wirklichkeit," *Historische Zeitschrift*, CLXXXI (1956).

Trials of the War Criminals before the Nuernberg Military Tribunals (14 vols., Nuremberg, 1946 ff.).

Turner, Henry L. *Stresemann and the Politics of the Weimar Republic* (Princeton, 1963).

Vallentin, Antonina. *Stresemann* (London, 1931).

Vossler, Otto. "Bismarcks Ethos," *Historische Zeitschrift*, CLXXI (1951).

Waldersee, Generalfeldmarschall Alfred Graf von. *Denkwürdigkeiten*, herausgegeben von H. O. Meisner (3 vols., Stuttgart, 1923-25).

Weber, Max. *From Max Weber: Essays in Sociology*, translated and edited by H. H. Gerth and C. Wright Mills (New York, 1946).

Weizsäcker, Ernst von. *Erinnerungen* (München, 1950).

Wertheimer, E. von. "Der Prozess Arnim," *Preussische Jahrbücher*, CCXXII (1930).

West German Leadership and Foreign Policy, edited by Hans Speier and W. Phillips Davison (Evanston, 1957).

Weymar, Paul. *Konrad Adenauer, die autorisierte Biographie* (München, 1955).

Widenmann, Wilhelm. *Marine-Attaché an der kaiserlich-deutschen Botschaft in London, 1907-1912* (Göttingen, 1952).

Windelband, Wolfgang. *Bismarck und die europäischen Grossmächte, 1879-1885* (Essen, 1940).

Woodward, E. L. *Great Britain and the German Navy* (Oxford, 1935).

Zechlin, Egmont. *Bismarck und die Grundlegung der deutschen Grossmacht* (Stuttgart, 1930).

Zedlitz-Trützscher, Graf. *Zwölf Jahre am deutschen Kaiserhof* (Berlin, 1924).

Zimmermann, Ludwig. *Studien zur Geschichte der Weimarer Republik* (Erlangen, 1956).

INDEX

Abetz, Otto, representative of the Ribbentrop Bureau in Paris, 90.

Adenauer, Konrad, as Chief Mayor of Cologne, 1917-33, 96-99, 101; as Chancellor, 1949-63, 100 ff., 106 ff.; personal qualities, 99 ff.; as negotiator, 98 ff.; on reconciliation with France, 108, 115 ff.; relations with the Soviet Union, 100, 103, 105, 111 ff.; and Bundestag, 103, 104, 112 f.; attitude toward Foreign Ministry and Foreign Service, 104-106; on re-unification of Germany, 106 ff., 112 f.; Moscow trip, 1955, 103 f., 105, 113.

Africa, 16.

Agadir crisis, 1911, 41.

Alexander the Great, 22.

Alexander II, Tsar of Russia, 24.

Alexander of Battenberg, Prince, 11 n.

Alliances and alignments: Dual Alliance of 1879, 17 n., 29, 35, 77; Franco-Russian Alliance, 1894, 31, 35, 36; *Entente cordiale*, 1904, 31, 55; Franco-Polish Alliance, 1920, 56; North Atlantic Alliance, 1949, 96.

Allied High Commission in Germany, 1949-55, 99 f., 104.

Alsace-Lorraine, 56.

Andrae-Roman, Alexander, 14.

Andreas, Willy, 40.

Angra Pequena, 1884, 77.

Anschluss, see Austria.

Army, Prussian and German: influence on foreign policy, x, 7, 18, 27, 31, 39, 59, 79, 81.

Arnim, Harry Count von, German ambassador, 8, 25, 74, 75, 76.

Augstein, Rudolf, 100.

Austria, 4, 6, 31, 41, 72; alliance with Germany, 1879-1918, 17 n., 29, 35, 39, 77; rivalry with Russia in the Balkans before

130

Format by Lydia Link
Set in Linotype Fairfield
HARPER & ROW, PUBLISHERS, INCORPORATED

harper ✦ torchbooks

HUMANITIES AND SOCIAL SCIENCES

American Studies: General

THOMAS C. COCHRAN: The Inner Revolution: *Essays on the Social Sciences in History* TB/1140

EDWARD S. CORWIN: American Constitutional History. △ *Essays edited by Alpheus T. Mason and Gerald Garvey* TB/1136

CARL N. DEGLER, Ed.: Pivotal Interpretations of American History TB/1240, TB/1241

A. HUNTER DUPREE: Science in the Federal Government: *A History of Politics and Activities to 1940* TB/573

A. S. EISENSTADT, Ed.: The Craft of American History: *Recent Essays in American Historical Writing* Vol. I TB/1255; Vol. II TB/1256

OSCAR HANDLIN, Ed.: This Was America: *As Recorded by European Travelers in the Eighteenth, Nineteenth and Twentieth Centuries. Illus.* TB/1119

MARCUS LEE HANSEN: The Atlantic Migration: 1607-1860. *Edited by Arthur M. Schlesinger* TB/1052

MARCUS LEE HANSEN: The Immigrant in American History. *Edited with a Foreword by Arthur M. Schlesinger* TB/1120

JOHN HIGHAM, Ed.: The Reconstruction of American History △ TB/1068

ROBERT H. JACKSON: The Supreme Court in the American System of Government TB/1106

JOHN F. KENNEDY: A Nation of Immigrants. △ *Illus.* TB/1118

RALPH BARTON PERRY: Puritanism and Democracy TB/1138

ARNOLD ROSE: The Negro in America: *The Condensed Version of Gunnar Myrdal's* An American Dilemma TB/3048

MAURICE R. STEIN: The Eclipse of Community: *An Interpretation of American Studies* TB/1128

W. LLOYD WARNER and Associates: Democracy in Jonesville: *A Study in Quality and Inequality* ¶ TB/1129

W. LLOYD WARNER: Social Class in America: *The Evaluation of Status* TB/1013

American Studies: Colonial

BERNARD BAILYN, Ed.: The Apologia of Robert Keayne: *Self-Portrait of a Puritan Merchant* TB/1201

BERNARD BAILYN: The New England Merchants in the Seventeenth Century TB/1149

JOSEPH CHARLES: The Origins of the American Party System TB/1049

LAWRENCE HENRY GIPSON: The Coming of the Revolution: 1763-1775. † *Illus.* TB/3007

LEONARD W. LEVY: Freedom of Speech and Press in Early American History: *Legacy of Suppression* TB/1109

PERRY MILLER: Errand Into the Wilderness TB/1139

PERRY MILLER & T. H. JOHNSON, Eds.: The Puritans: *A Sourcebook* Vol. I TB/1093; Vol. II TB/1094

EDMUND S. MORGAN, Ed.: The Diary of Michael Wigglesworth, 1653-1657: *The Conscience of a Puritan* TB/1228

EDMUND S. MORGAN: The Puritan Family: *Religion and Domestic Relations in Seventeenth-Century New England* TB/1227

RICHARD B. MORRIS: Government and Labor in Early America TB/1244

KENNETH B. MURDOCK: Literature and Theology in Colonial New England TB/99

WALLACE NOTESTEIN: The English People on the Eve of Colonization: 1603-1630. † *Illus.* TB/3006

LOUIS B. WRIGHT: The Cultural Life of the American Colonies: 1607-1763. † *Illus.* TB/3005

American Studies: From the Revolution to 1860

JOHN R. ALDEN: The American Revolution: 1775-1783. † *Illus.* TB/3011

MAX BELOFF, Ed.: The Debate on the American Revolution, 1761-1783: *A Sourcebook* △ TB/1225

RAY A. BILLINGTON: The Far Western Frontier: 1830-1860. † *Illus.* TB/3012

EDMUND BURKE: On the American Revolution. ‡ *Edited by Elliott Robert Barkan* TB/3068

WHITNEY R. CROSS: The Burned-Over District: *The Social and Intellectual History of Enthusiastic Religion in Western New York, 1800-1850* TB/1242

GEORGE DANGERFIELD: The Awakening of American Nationalism: 1815-1828. † *Illus.* TB/3061

CLEMENT EATON: The Freedom-of-Thought Struggle in the Old South. *Revised and Enlarged. Illus.* TB/1150

CLEMENT EATON: The Growth of Southern Civilization: 1790-1860. † *Illus.* TB/3040

LOUIS FILLER: The Crusade Against Slavery: 1830-1860. † *Illus.* TB/3029

DIXON RYAN FOX: The Decline of Aristocracy in the Politics of New York: 1801-1840. ‡ *Edited by Robert V. Remini* TB/3064

FELIX GILBERT: The Beginnings of American Foreign Policy: *To the Farewell Address* TB/1200

FRANCIS GRIERSON: The Valley of Shadows: *The Coming of the Civil War in Lincoln's Midwest: A Contemporary Account* TB/1246

FRANCIS J. GRUND: Aristocracy in America: *Social Class in the Formative Years of the New Nation* TB/1001

ALEXANDER HAMILTON: The Reports of Alexander Hamilton. ‡ *Edited by Jacob E. Cooke* TB/3060

---

† The New American Nation Series, edited by Henry Steele Commager and Richard B. Morris.

‡ American Perspectives series, edited by Bernard Wishy and William E. Leuchtenburg.

* The Rise of Modern Europe series, edited by William L. Langer.

¶ Researches in the Social, Cultural, and Behavioral Sciences, edited by Benjamin Nelson.

§ The Library of Religion and Culture, edited by Benjamin Nelson.

Σ Harper Modern Science Series, edited by James R. Newman.

º Not for sale in Canada.

△ Not for sale in the U. K.

THOMAS JEFFERSON: Notes on the State of Virginia. ‡ Edited by Thomas P. Abernethy TB/3052
JAMES MADISON: The Forging of American Federalism: Selected Writings of James Madison. Edited by Saul K. Padover TB/1126
BERNARD MAYO: Myths and Men: Patrick Henry, George Washington, Thomas Jefferson TB/1108
JOHN C. MILLER: Alexander Hamilton and the Growth of the New Nation TB/3057
RICHARD B. MORRIS, Ed.: The Era of the American Revolution TB/1180
R. B. NYE: The Cultural Life of the New Nation: 1776-1801. † Illus. TB/3026
FRANCIS S. PHILBRICK: The Rise of the West, 1754-1830. † Illus. TB/3067
TIMOTHY L. SMITH: Revivalism and Social Reform: American Protestantism on the Eve of the Civil War TB/1229
FRANK THISTLETHWAITE: America and the Atlantic Community: Anglo-American Aspects, 1790-1850 TB/1107
A. F. TYLER: Freedom's Ferment: Phases of American Social History from the Revolution to the Outbreak of the Civil War. 31 illus. TB/1074
GLYNDON G. VAN DEUSEN: The Jacksonian Era: 1828-1848. † Illus. TB/3028
LOUIS B. WRIGHT: Culture on the Moving Frontier TB/1053

American Studies: The Civil War to 1900

THOMAS C. COCHRAN & WILLIAM MILLER: The Age of Enterprise: A Social History of Industrial America TB/1054
W. A. DUNNING: Essays on the Civil War and Reconstruction. Introduction by David Donald TB/1181
W. A. DUNNING: Reconstruction, Political and Economic: 1865-1877 TB/1073
HAROLD U. FAULKNER: Politics, Reform and Expansion: 1890-1900. † Illus. TB/3020
HELEN HUNT JACKSON: A Century of Dishonor: The Early Crusade for Indian Reform. ‡ Edited by Andrew F. Rolle TB/3063
ALBERT D. KIRWAN: Revolt of the Rednecks: Mississippi Politics, 1876-1925 TB/1199
ROBERT GREEN MC CLOSKEY: American Conservatism in the Age of Enterprise: 1865-1910 TB/1137
ARTHUR MANN: Yankee Reformers in the Urban Age: Social Reform in Boston, 1880-1900 TB/1247
WHITELAW REID: After the War: A Tour of the Southern States, 1865-1866. ‡ Edited by C. Vann Woodward TB/3066
CHARLES H. SHINN: Mining Camps: A Study in American Frontier Government. ‡ Edited by Rodman W. Paul TB/3062
VERNON LANE WHARTON: The Negro in Mississippi: 1865-1890 TB/1178

American Studies: 1900 to the Present

RAY STANNARD BAKER: Following the Color Line: American Negro Citizenship in Progressive Era. ‡ Illus. Edited by Dewey W. Grantham, Jr. TB/3053
RANDOLPH S. BOURNE: War and the Intellectuals: Collected Essays, 1915-1919. ‡ Ed. by Carl Resek TB/3043
A. RUSSELL BUCHANAN: The United States and World War II. † Illus. Vol. I TB/3044; Vol. II TB/3045
ABRAHAM CAHAN: The Rise of David Levinsky: a documentary novel of social mobility in early twentieth century America. Intro. by John Higham TB/1028
THOMAS C. COCHRAN: The American Business System: A Historical Perspective, 1900-1955 TB/1080
FOSTER RHEA DULLES: America's Rise to World Power: 1898-1954. † Illus. TB/3021
JOHN D. HICKS: Republican Ascendancy: 1921-1933. † Illus. TB/3041
SIDNEY HOOK: Reason, Social Myths, and Democracy TB/1237
ROBERT HUNTER: Poverty: Social Conscience in the Progressive Era. ‡ Edited by Peter d'A. Jones TB/3065

WILLIAM L. LANGER & S. EVERETT GLEASON: The Challenge to Isolation: The World Crisis of 1937-1940 and American Foreign Policy
Vol. I TB/3054; Vol. II TB/3055
WILLIAM E. LEUCHTENBURG: Franklin D. Roosevelt and the New Deal: 1932-1940. † Illus. TB/3025
ARTHUR S. LINK: Woodrow Wilson and the Progressive Era: 1910-1917. † Illus. TB/3023
GEORGE E. MOWRY: The Era of Theodore Roosevelt and the Birth of Modern America: 1900-1912. † TB/3022
RUSSEL B. NYE: Midwestern Progressive Politics TB/1202
WALTER RAUSCHENBUSCH: Christianity and the Social Crisis. ‡ Edited by Robert D. Cross TB/3059
JACOB RIIS: The Making of an American. ‡ Edited by Roy Lubove TB/3070
PHILIP SELZNICK: TVA and the Grass Roots: A Study in the Sociology of Formal Organization TB/1230
IDA M. TARBELL: The History of the Standard Oil Company. Briefer Version. ‡ Edited by David M. Chalmers TB/3071
GEORGE B. TINDALL, Ed.: A Populist Reader ‡ TB/3069
TWELVE SOUTHERNERS: I'll Take My Stand: The South and the Agrarian Tradition. Intro. by Louis D. Rubin, Jr. Biographical Essays by Virginia Rock TB/1072
WALTER E. WEYL: The New Democracy: An Essay on Certain Political Tendencies in the United States. ‡ Edited by Charles B. Forcey TB/3042

Anthropology

JACQUES BARZUN: Race: A Study in Superstition. Revised Edition TB/1172
JOSEPH B. CASAGRANDE, Ed.: In the Company of Man: Portraits of Anthropological Informants TB/3047
W. E. LE GROS CLARK: The Antecedents of Man: Intro. to Evolution of the Primates. o △ Illus. TB/559
CORA DU BOIS: The People of Alor. New Preface by the author. Illus. Vol. I TB/1042; Vol. II TB/1043
RAYMOND FIRTH, Ed.: Man and Culture: An Evaluation of the Work of Bronislaw Malinowski o △ TB/1133
DAVID LANDY: Tropical Childhood: Cultural Transmission and Learning in a Puerto Rican Village ¶ TB/1235
L. S. B. LEAKEY: Adam's Ancestors: The Evolution of Man and His Culture. △ Illus. TB/1019
ROBERT H. LOWIE: Primitive Society. Introduction by Fred Eggan TB/1056
EDWARD BURNETT TYLOR: The Origin of Culture. Part I of "Primitive Culture." § Intro. by Paul Radin TB/33
EDWARD BURNETT TYLOR: Religion in Primitive Culture. Part II of "Primitive Culture." § Intro. by Paul Radin TB/34
W. LLOYD WARNER: A Black Civilization: A Study of an Australian Tribe. ¶ Illus. TB/3056

Art and Art History

WALTER LOWRIE: Art in the Early Church. Revised Edition. 452 illus. TB/124
EMILE MÂLE: The Gothic Image: Religious Art in France of the Thirteenth Century. § △ 190 illus. TB/44
MILLARD MEISS: Painting in Florence and Siena after the Black Death: The Arts, Religion and Society in the Mid-Fourteenth Century. 169 illus. TB/1148
ERICH NEUMANN: The Archetypal World of Henry Moore. △ 107 illus. TB/2020
DORA & ERWIN PANOFSKY: Pandora's Box: The Changing Aspects of a Mythical Symbol. Illus. TB/2021
ERWIN PANOFSKY: Studies in Iconology: Humanistic Themes in the Art of the Renaissance. △ 180 illustrations TB/1077
ALEXANDRE PIANKOFF: The Shrines of Tut-Ankh-Amon. Edited by N. Rambova. 117 illus. TB/2011
JEAN SEZNEC: The Survival of the Pagan Gods △ TB/2004
OTTO VON SIMSON: The Gothic Cathedral △ TB/2018
HEINRICH ZIMMER: Myths and Symbols in Indian Art and Civilization. 70 illustrations TB/2005

Business, Economics & Economic History

REINHARD BENDIX: Work and Authority in Industry
TB/3035
GILBERT BURCK & EDITORS OF FORTUNE: The Computer
Age: And Its Potential for Management   TB/1179
THOMAS C. COCHRAN: The American Business System: A
Historical Perspective, 1900-1955   TB/1080
THOMAS C. COCHRAN: The Inner Revolution: Essays on
the Social Sciences in History   TB/1140
THOMAS C. COCHRAN & WILLIAM MILLER: The Age of Enter-
prise: A Social History of Industrial America TB/1054
ROBERT DAHL & CHARLES E. LINDBLOM: Politics, Eco-
nomics, and Welfare   TB/3037
PETER F. DRUCKER: The New Society: The Anatomy of
Industrial Order △   TB/1082
EDITORS OF FORTUNE: America in the Sixties: The Econ-
omy and the Society   TB/1015
ROBERT L. HEILBRONER: The Great Ascent: The Struggle
for Economic Development in Our Time   TB/3030
FRANK H. KNIGHT: The Economic Organization TB/1214
FRANK H. KNIGHT: Risk, Uncertainty and Profit TB/1215
ABBA P. LERNER: Everybody's Business   TB/3051
ROBERT GREEN MC CLOSKEY: American Conservatism in
the Age of Enterprise, 1865-1910   TB/1137
PAUL MANTOUX: The Industrial Revolution in the
Eighteenth Century ○ △   TB/1079
WILLIAM MILLER, Ed.: Men in Business: Essays on the
Historical Role of the Entrepreneur   TB/1081
RICHARD B. MORRIS: Government and Labor in Early
America   TB/1244
HERBERT SIMON: The Shape of Automation: For Men and
Management   TB/1245
PERRIN STRYKER: The Character of the Executive: Eleven
Studies in Managerial Qualities   TB/1041
PIERRE URI: Partnership for Progress: A Program for
Transatlantic Action   TB/3036

Contemporary Culture

JACQUES BARZUN: The House of Intellect △   TB/1051
CLARK KERR: The Uses of the University   TB/1264
JOHN U. NEF: Cultural Foundations of Industrial Civi-
lization △   TB/1024
NATHAN M. PUSEY: The Age of the Scholar: Observations
on Education in a Troubled Decade   TB/1157
PAUL VALÉRY: The Outlook for Intelligence △   TB/2016
RAYMOND WILLIAMS: Culture and Society, 1780-1950 ○ △
TB/1252
RAYMOND WILLIAMS: The Long Revolution.○ △ Revised
Edition   TB/1253

Historiography & Philosophy of History

JACOB BURCKHARDT: On History and Historians. △ Intro-
duction by H. R. Trevor-Roper   TB/1216
WILHELM DILTHEY: Pattern and Meaning in History:
Thoughts on History and Society. ○ △ Edited with an
Introduction by H. P. Rickman   TB/1075
J. H. HEXTER: Reappraisals in History: New Views on
History & Society in Early Modern Europe △ TB/1100
H. STUART HUGHES: History as Art and as Science: Twin
Vistas on the Past   TB/1207
RAYMOND KLIBANSKY & H. J. PATON, Eds.: Philosophy and
History: The Ernst Cassirer Festschrift. Illus.
TB/1115
GEORGE H. NADEL, Ed.: Studies in the Philosophy of His-
tory: Essays from History and Theory   TB/1208
JOSE ORTEGA Y GASSET: The Modern Theme. Introduc-
tion by Jose Ferrater Mora   TB/1038
KARL R. POPPER: The Open Society and Its Enemies △
Vol. I: The Spell of Plato   TB/1101
Vol. II: The High Tide of Prophecy: Hegel, Marx and
the Aftermath   TB/1102
KARL R. POPPER: The Poverty of Historicism ○ △ TB/1126
G. J. RENIER: History: Its Purpose and Method △ TB/1209
W. H. WALSH: Philosophy of History △   TB/1020

History: General

L. CARRINGTON GOODRICH: A Short History of the Chinese People. △ Illus.   TB/3015
DAN N. JACOBS & HANS H. BAERWALD: Chinese Communism: Selected Documents   TB/3031
BERNARD LEWIS: The Arabs in History △   TB/1029

History: Ancient

A. ANDREWES: The Greek Tyrants △   TB/1103
ADOLF ERMAN, Ed.: The Ancient Egyptians   TB/1233
MICHAEL GRANT: Ancient History ○ △   TB/1190
SAMUEL NOAH KRAMER: Sumerian Mythology   TB/1055
NAPHTALI LEWIS & MEYER REINHOLD, Eds.: Roman Civili-
zation. Sourcebook I: The Republic   TB/1231
NAPHTALI LEWIS & MEYER REINHOLD, Eds.: Roman Civili-
zation. Sourcebook II: The Empire   TB/1232

History: Medieval

P. BOISSONNADE: Life and Work in Medieval Europe ○ △
TB/1141
HELEN CAM: England before Elizabeth △   TB/1026
NORMAN COHN: The Pursuit of the Millennium △ TB/1037
G. G. COULTON: Medieval Village, Manor, and Monastery
TB/1022
CHRISTOPHR DAWSON, Ed.: Mission to Asia: Narratives
and Letters of the Franciscan Missionaries in Mon-
golia and China in the 13th and 14th Centuries △
TB/315
HEINRICH FICHTENAU: The Carolingian Empire: The Age
of Charlemagne △   TB/1142
F. L. GANSHOF: Feudalism △   TB/1058
DENO GEANAKOPLOS: Byzantine East and Latin West:
Two Worlds of Christendom in Middle Ages and
Renaissance △   TB/1265
EDWARD GIBBON: The Triumph of Christendom in the
Roman Empire (Chaps. XV-XX of "Decline and Fall,"
J. B. Bury edition). § △ Illus.   TB/46
W. O. HASSALL, Ed.: Medieval England: As Viewed by
Contemporaries △   TB/1205
DENYS HAY: The Medieval Centuries ○ △   TB/1192
J. M. HUSSEY: The Byzantine World △   TB/1057
FERDINAND LOT: The End of the Ancient World and the
Beginnings of the Middle Ages   TB/1044
G. MOLLAT: The Popes at Avignon: 1305-1378 △ TB/308
CHARLES PETIT-DUTAILLIS: The Feudal Monarchy in
France and England ○ △   TB/1165
HENRI PIRENNE: Early Democracies in the Low Coun-
tries   TB/1110
STEVEN RUNCIMAN: A History of the Crusades. △
Volume I: The First Crusade and the Foundation of
the Kingdom of Jerusalem. Illus.   TB/1143
Volume II: The Kingdom of Jerusalem and the
Frankish East, 1100-1187. Illus.   TB/1243
FERDINAND SCHEVILL: Siena: The History of a Medieval
Commune. Intro. by William M. Bowsky   TB/1164
SULPICIUS SEVERUS et al.: The Western Fathers: Being
the Lives of Martin of Tours, Ambrose, Augustine of
Hippo, Honoratus of Arles and Germanus of Aux-
erre. △ Edited and translated by F. R. Hoare TB/309
HENRY OSBORN TAYLOR: The Classical Heritage of the
Middle Ages   TB/1117
F. VAN DER MEER: Augustine the Bishop: Church and
Society at the Dawn of the Middle Ages △   TB/304
J. M. WALLACE-HADRILL: The Barbarian West: The Early
Middle Ages, A.D. 400-1000 △   TB/1061

History: Renaissance & Reformation

JACOB BURCKHARDT: The Civilization of the Renaissance
in Italy. △ Illus.   Vol. I TB/40; Vol. II TB/41
JOHN CALVIN & JACOPO SADOLETO: A Reformation Debate.
Edited by John C. Olin   TB/1239

3

ERNST CASSIRER: The Individual and the Cosmos in Renaissance Philosophy. △ *Translated with an Introduction by Mario Domandi*   TB/1097

FEDERICO CHABOD: Machiavelli & Renaissance △ TB/1193

EDWARD P. CHEYNEY: The Dawn of a New Era, 1250-1453. * *Illus.*   TB/3002

G. CONSTANT: The Reformation in England: *The English Schism, Henry VIII, 1509-1547* △   TB/314

R. TREVOR DAVIES: The Golden Century of Spain, 1501-1621 ° △   TB/1194

DESIDERIUS ERASMUS: Christian Humanism and the Reformation: *Selected Writings. Edited and translated by John C. Olin*   TB/1166

WALLACE K. FERGUSON et al.: Facets of the Renaissance   TB/1098

WALLACE K. FERGUSON et al.: The Renaissance: *Six Essays. Illus.*   TB/1084

JOHN NEVILLE FIGGIS: The Divine Right of Kings. *Introduction by G. R. Elton*   TB/1191

JOHN NEVILLE FIGGIS: Political Thought from Gerson to Grotius: 1414-1625   TB/1032

MYRON P. GILMORE: The World of Humanism, 1453-1517. * *Illus.*   TB/3003

FRANCESCO GUICCIARDINI: Maxims and Reflections of a Renaissance Statesman (*Ricordi*)   TB/1160

J. H. HEXTER: More's Utopia: *The Biography of an Idea. New Epilogue by the Author*   TB/1195

HAJO HOLBORN: Ulrich von Hutten and the German Reformation   TB/1238

JOHAN HUIZINGA: Erasmus and the Age of Reformation.△ *Illus.*   TB/19

JOEL HURSTFIELD, Ed.: The Reformation Crisis △ TB/1267

ULRICH VON HUTTEN et al.: On the Eve of the Reformation: *"Letters of Obscure Men"*   TB/1124

PAUL O. KRISTELLER: Renaissance Thought: *The Classic, Scholastic, and Humanist Strains*   TB/1048

PAUL O. KRISTELLER: Renaissance Thought II: *Papers on Humanism and the Arts*   TB/1163

NICCOLO MACHIAVELLI: History of Florence and of the Affairs of Italy   TB/1027

ALFRED VON MARTIN: Sociology of the Renaissance. *Introduction by Wallace K. Ferguson* △   TB/1099

GARRETT MATTINGLY et al.: Renaissance Profiles. △ *Edited by J. H. Plumb*   TB/1162

MILLARD MEISS: Painting in Florence and Siena after the Black Death: *The Arts, Religion and Society in the Mid-Fourteenth Century.* △ *169 illus.*   TB/1148

J. E. NEALE: The Age of Catherine de Medici ° △ TB/1085

ERWIN PANOFSKY: Studies in Iconology: *Humanistic Themes in the Art of the Renaissance* △   TB/1077

J. H. PARRY: The Establishment of the European Hegemony: 1415-1715 △   TB/1045

J. H. PLUMB: The Italian Renaissance: *A Concise Survey of Its History and Culture* △   TB/1161

A. F. POLLARD: Henry VIII. ° △ *Introduction by A. G. Dickens*   TB/1249

A. F. POLLARD: Wolsey. ° △ *Introduction by A. G. Dickens*   TB/1248

CECIL ROTH: The Jews in the Renaissance. *Illus.* TB/834

A. L. ROWSE: The Expansion of Elizabethan England. ° △ *Illus.*   TB/1220

GORDON RUPP: Luther's Progress to the Diet of Worms ° △   TB/120

FERDINAND SCHEVILL: The Medici. *Illus.*   TB/1010

FERDINAND SCHEVILL: Medieval and Renaissance Florence. *Illus.*   Volume I: *Medieval Florence* TB/1090 Volume II: *The Coming of Humanism and the Age of the Medici*   TB/1091

G. M. TREVELYAN: England in the Age of Wycliffe, 1368-1520 ° △   TB/1112

VESPASIANO: Renaissance Princes, Popes, and Prelates: *The Vespasiano Memoirs: Lives of Illustrious Men of the XVth Century*   TB/1111

FREDERICK B. ARTZ: Reaction and Revolution, 1815-1852. * *Illus.*   TB/3034

MAX BELOFF: The Age of Absolutism, 1660-1815 △ TB/1062

ROBERT C. BINKLEY: Realism and Nationalism, 1852-1871. * *Illus.*   TB/3038

ASA BRIGGS: The Making of Modern England, 1784-1867: *The Age of Improvement* ° △   TB/1203

CRANE BRINTON: A Decade of Revolution, 1789-1799. * *Illus.*   TB/3018

D. W. BROGAN: The Development of Modern France. ° △ Volume I: *From the Fall of the Empire to the Dreyfus Affair*   TB/1184 Volume II: *The Shadow of War, World War I, Between the Two Wars. New Introduction by the Author*   TB/1185

J. BRONOWSKI & BRUCE MAZLISH: The Western Intellectual Tradition: *From Leonardo to Hegel* △ TB/3001

GEOFFREY BRUUN: Europe and the French Imperium, 1799-1814. * *Illus.*   TB/3033

ALAN BULLOCK: Hitler, A Study in Tyranny ° △ TB/1123

E. H. CARR: The Twenty Years' Crisis, 1919-1939 ° △   TB/1122

GORDON A. CRAIG: From Bismarck to Adenauer: *Aspects of German Statecraft. Revised Edition* TB/1171

WALTER L. DORN: Competition for Empire, 1740-1763. * *Illus.*   TB/3032

FRANKLIN L. FORD: Robe and Sword: *The Regrouping of the French Aristocracy after Louis XIV* TB/1217

CARL J. FRIEDRICH: The Age of the Baroque, 1610-1660. * *Illus.*   TB/3004

RENÉ FUELOEP-MILLER: The Mind and Face of Bolshevism   TB/1188

M. DOROTHY GEORGE: London Life in the Eighteenth Century △   TB/1182

LEO GERSHOY: From Despotism to Revolution, 1763-1789. * *Illus.*   TB/3017

C. C. GILLISPIE: Genesis and Geology: *The Decades before Darwin* §   TB/51

ALBERT GOODWIN: The French Revolution △   TB/1064

ALBERT GUÉRARD: France in the Classical Age: *The Life and Death of an Ideal* △   TB/1183

CARLTON J. H. HAYES: A Generation of Materialism, 1871-1900. * *Illus.*   TB/3039

J. H. HEXTER: Reappraisals in History: *New Views on History & Society in Early Modern Europe* △ TB/1100

STANLEY HOFFMANN et al.: In Search of France   TB/1219

A. R. HUMPHREYS: The Augustan World: *Society, Thought, and Letters in 18th Century England* ° △ TB/1105

DAN N. JACOBS, Ed.: The New Communist Manifesto & Related Documents. Third edition, *Revised* TB/1078

HANS KOHN: The Mind of Germany △   TB/1204

HANS KOHN, Ed.: The Mind of Modern Russia: *Historical and Political Thought of Russia's Great Age* TB/1065

FRANK E. MANUEL: The Prophets of Paris: *Turgot, Condorcet, Saint-Simon, Fourier, and Comte* TB/1218

KINGSLEY MARTIN: French Liberal Thought in the Eighteenth Century   TB/1114

L. B. NAMIER: Personalities and Powers: *Selected Essays* △   TB/1186

L. B. NAMIER: Vanished Supremacies: *Essays on European History, 1812-1918* ° △   TB/1088

JOHN U. NEF: Western Civilization Since the Renaissance: *Peace, War, Industry, and the Arts* TB/1113

FREDERICK L. NUSSBAUM: The Triumph of Science and Reason, 1660-1685. * *Illus.*   TB/3009

JOHN PLAMENATZ: German Marxism and Russian Communism. ° △ *New Preface by the Author*   TB/1189

RAYMOND W. POSTGATE, Ed.: Revolution from 1789 to 1906: *Selected Documents*   TB/1063

PENFIELD ROBERTS: The Quest for Security, 1715-1740. * *Illus.*   TB/3016

PRISCILLA ROBERTSON: Revolutions of 1848: A Social History TB/1025
LOUIS, DUC DE SAINT-SIMON: Versailles, The Court, and Louis XIV. △ Introductory Note by Peter Gay TB/1250
ALBERT SOREL: Europe Under the Old Regime. Translated by Francis H. Herrick TB/1121
N. N. SUKHANOV: The Russian Revolution, 1917: Eyewitness Account. △ Edited by Joel Carmichael
  Vol. I TB/1066; Vol. II TB/1067
A. J. P. TAYLOR: From Napoleon to Lenin: Historical Essays o △ TB/1268
A. J. P. TAYLOR: The Habsburg Monarchy, 1809-1918 o △
  TB/1187
G. M. TREVELYAN: British History in the Nineteenth Century and After: 1782-1919. △ Second Edition
  TB/1251
H. R. TREVOR-ROPER: Historical Essays o △ TB/1269
JOHN B. WOLF: The Emergence of the Great Powers, 1685-1715. * Illus. TB/3010
JOHN B. WOLF: France: 1814-1919: The Rise of a Liberal-Democratic Society TB/3019

Intellectual History & History of Ideas

HERSCHEL BAKER: The Image of Man TB/1047
R. R. BOLGAR: The Classical Heritage and Its Beneficiaries △ TB/1125
RANDOLPH S. BOURNE: War and the Intellectuals: Collected Essays, 1915-1919. ‡ △ Edited by Carl Resek
  TB/3043
J. BRONOWSKI & BRUCE MAZLISH: The Western Intellectual Tradition: From Leonardo to Hegel △ TB/3001
ERNST CASSIRER: The Individual and the Cosmos in Renaissance Philosophy. △ Translated with an Introduction by Mario Domandi TB/1097
NORMAN COHN: Pursuit of the Millennium △ TB/1037
C. C. GILLISPIE: Genesis and Geology: The Decades before Darwin § TB/51
G. RACHEL LEVY: Religious Conceptions of the Stone Age and Their Influence upon European Thought. △ Illus. Introduction by Henri Frankfort TB/106
ARTHUR O. LOVEJOY: The Great Chain of Being: A Study of the History of an Idea TB/1009
FRANK E. MANUEL: The Prophets of Paris: Turgot, Condorcet, Saint-Simon, Fourier, and Comte TB/1218
PERRY MILLER & T. H. JOHNSON, Editors: The Puritans: A Sourcebook of Their Writings
  Vol. I TB/1093; Vol. II TB/1094
MILTON C. NAHM: Genius and Creativity: An Essay in the History of Ideas TB/1196
ROBERT PAYNE: Hubris: A Study of Pride. Foreword by Sir Herbert Read TB/1031
RALPH BARTON PERRY: The Thought and Character of William James: Briefer Version TB/1156
GEORG SIMMEL et al.: Essays on Sociology, Philosophy, and Aesthetics. ¶ Edited by Kurt H. Wolff TB/1234
BRUNO SNELL: The Discovery of the Mind: The Greek Origins of European Thought △ TB/1018
PAGET TOYNBEE: Dante Alighieri: His Life and Works. Edited with Intro. by Charles S. Singleton TB/1206
ERNEST LEE TUVESON: Millennium and Utopia: A Study in the Background of the Idea of Progress. ¶ New Preface by the Author TB/1134
PAUL VALÉRY: The Outlook for Intelligence △ TB/2016
PHILIP P. WIENER: Evolution and the Founders of Pragmatism. △ Foreword by John Dewey TB/1212
BASIL WILLEY: Nineteenth Century Studies: Coleridge to Matthew Arnold o △ TB/1261
BASIL WILLEY: More Nineteenth Century Studies: A Group of Honest Doubters o △ TB/1262

Literature, Poetry, The Novel & Criticism

JACQUES BARZUN: The House of Intellect △ TB/1051
W. J. BATE: From Classic to Romantic: Premises of Taste in Eighteenth Century England TB/1036
RACHEL BESPALOFF: On the Iliad TB/2006

R. P. BLACKMUR et al.: Lectures in Criticism. Introduction by Huntington Cairns TB/2003
JAMES BOSWELL: The Life of Dr. Johnson & The Journal of a Tour to the Hebrides with Samuel Johnson LL.D: Selections. o △ Edited by F. V. Morley. Illus. by Ernest Shepard TB/1254
ABRAHAM CAHAN: The Rise of David Levinsky: a documentary novel of social mobility in early twentieth century America. Intro. by John Higham TB/1028
ERNST R. CURTIUS: European Literature and the Latin Middle Ages △ TB/2015
GEORGE ELIOT: Daniel Deronda TB/1039
ÉTIENNE GILSON: Dante and Philosophy TB/1089
ALFRED HARBAGE: As They Liked It: A Study of Shakespeare's Moral Artistry TB/1035
STANLEY R. HOPPER, Ed.: Spiritual Problems in Contemporary Literature § TB/21
A. R. HUMPHREYS: The Augustan World: Society in 18th Century England o △ TB/1105
ALDOUS HUXLEY: Antic Hay & The Giaconda Smile. o △ Introduction by Martin Green TB/3503
ALDOUS HUXLEY: Brave New World & Brave New World Revisited. o △ Introduction by Martin Green TB/3501
HENRY JAMES: The Tragic Muse TB/1017
ARNOLD KETTLE: An Introduction to the English Novel △
  Volume I: Defoe to George Eliot TB/1011
  Volume II: Henry James to the Present TB/1012
RICHMOND LATTIMORE: The Poetry of Greek Tragedy △
  TB/1257
J. B. LEISHMAN: The Monarch of Wit: An Analytical and Comparative Study of the Poetry of John Donne o △
  TB/1258
J. B. LEISHMAN: Themes and Variations in Shakespeare's Sonnets o △ TB/1259
ROGER SHERMAN LOOMIS: The Development of Arthurian Romance △ TB/1167
JOHN STUART MILL: On Bentham and Coleridge. △ Introduction by F. R. Leavis TB/1070
KENNETH B. MURDOCK: Literature and Theology in Colonial New England TB/99
SAMUEL PEPYS: The Diary of Samuel Pepys. o Edited by O. F. Morshead. Illus. by Ernest Shepard TB/1007
ST.-JOHN PERSE: Seamarks TB/2002
V. DE S. PINTO: Crisis in English Poetry, 1880-1940 o △
  TB/1260
GEORGE SANTAYANA: Interpretations of Poetry and Religion § TB/9
C. K. STEAD: The New Poetic: Yeats to Eliot o △ TB/1263
HEINRICH STRAUMANN: American Literature in the Twentieth Century. △ Third Edition, Revised TB/1168
PAGET TOYNBEE: Dante Alighieri: His Life and Works. Edited with Intro. by Charles S. Singleton TB/1206
DOROTHY VAN GHENT: The English Novel TB/1050
E. B. WHITE: One Man's Meat TB/3505
BASIL WILLEY: Nineteenth Century Studies: Coleridge to Matthew Arnold o △ TB/1261
BASIL WILLEY: More Nineteenth Century Studies: A Group of Honest Doubters o △ TB/1262
RAYMOND WILLIAMS: Culture and Society, 1780-1950 △
  TB/1252
RAYMOND WILLIAMS: The Long Revolution. △ Revised Edition TB/1253
MORTON DAUWEN ZABEL, Editor: Literary Opinion in America Vol. I TB/3013; Vol. II TB/3014

Myth, Symbol & Folklore

JOSEPH CAMPBELL, Editor: Pagan and Christian Mysteries. Illus. TB/2013
MIRCEA ELIADE: Cosmos and History: The Myth of the Eternal Return § △ TB/2050
MIRCEA ELIADE: Rites and Symbols of Initiation: The Mysteries of Birth and Rebirth § △ TB/1236

5

Philosophy

Political Science & Government

Psychology